GHANA LANDS IN FOCUS
VOLUME 1

ENGR. E. A GYAMERA (PHD)

Copyright © 2022 by Engr. E. A Gyamera (PhD).

ISBN:	Softcover	978-1-5437-7217-3
	eBook	978-1-5437-7216-6

All rights reserved. No part of this book may be used or reproduced by any means, graphic, electronic, or mechanical, including photocopying, recording, taping or by any information storage retrieval system without the written permission of the author except in the case of brief quotations embodied in critical articles and reviews.

Scripture quotations marked NKJV are taken from the New King James Version. Copyright © 1982 by Thomas Nelson, Inc. Used by permission. All rights reserved.

Because of the dynamic nature of the Internet, any web addresses or links contained in this book may have changed since publication and may no longer be valid. The views expressed in this work are solely those of the author and do not necessarily reflect the views of the publisher, and the publisher hereby disclaims any responsibility for them.

Print information available on the last page.

To order additional copies of this book, contact
Toll Free +65 3165 7531 (Singapore)
Toll Free +60 3 3099 4412 (Malaysia)
orders.singapore@partridgepublishing.com

www.partridgepublishing.com/singapore

DEDICATION

This book is kindly dedicated to the *seniors* in the profession of *land surveying*.

ACKNOWLEDGEMENT

I will love the Lord with all my heart and worship him with humility, for if not him, I wouldn't have been raised from the dust to a fertile ground. May his name be praised for ever and ever. Amen.

I would like to sincerely appreciate Pastor Partrick Obeng Gyamera, author of the amazing book, *Who Is Jesus to You*, for his immense contribution towards the making of this book. God bless you, my brother. To my mom, Mrs. Mary Gyamera, and my wife, Mrs. Adjoa Gyamera, I can't quantify my appreciation to you for having been supportive in prayers, love, and affection.

My profound gratitude also goes to Dr Gifty Gyamera (GIMPA), Dr Stephen Laryea (Cape Coast Teaching Hospital), Mr. Williams Osei (UCC), Mr. Emmanuel Owusu (HOME BOUND), Mme. Ama Marfo (Cape Tech), Mr. Gilbert Osei (UCC), and Eng. Akwasi Twum Agyakwa (GYAM Eng. & Const. LTD) for their constructive criticism, which contributed to the status of this book.

To all my fans out there, thank you so much.
God bless you all.

CONTENTS

List of Figures xiii
Foreword xv
Introduction xix

Chapter 1 Land Holdings and Land Tenure System
            in Ghana 1
            1.1 Land Tenure System in Ghana 2
                 1.1.1 Landownership in Ghana 2
                 1.1.2 Land Acquisition in Ghana 9
                 1.1.3 Types of Land Agreement or Indenture 14
            1.2 Why People Encounter Problems in
                Land Acquisition 15
            1.3 Deed and Title Registration in Ghana 15
                 1.3.1 Deed Registration 15
                 1.3.2 Title Registration 17
            1.4 Limitations of Title Registration 18
            1.5 Challenges in the Land Sector 19
            1.6 The Way Forward 20
Chapter 2 Land Surveying in Ghana 23
            2.1 Surveying and Technology 24
                 2.1.1 Who Is a Professional Surveyor? 24
                 2.1.2 The Difference amongst Licenced,
                       Registered, or Professional Surveyor 25
                 2.1.3 The Work of a Land Surveyor 25
                 2.1.4 Careers in the Profession of Land
                       Surveying 26
                 2.1.5 Practising Cadastral Land Surveying
                       in Ghana 27
                 2.1.6 Practising Surveying without a Licence 28

  2.1.7 Having a Complaint about a Land Surveyor..................29
 2.2 How Land Survey Affects Human Life 29
Chapter 3 The Need of a Surveyor 32
 3.1 Some Departments and Agencies Land Surveyors Work For..33
 3.2 Types of Land Surveys.....................................34
 3.3 Why and When Would I Need a Land Surveyor?...39
 3.4 What a Land Surveyor Could Do for You.......40
  3.4.1 What You Should Know or Ask When Hiring a Land Surveyor...................41
 3.5 Information You Should Supply the Land Surveyor 43
 3.6 What Does the Land Surveyor Do When You Hire Him/Her? 44
 3.7 What Do You Get from a Land Surveyor? 45
 3.8 Should the Land Surveyor Tell You What You Own?..45
 3.9 Will You Be Shown Your Property Corners and Lines by the Surveyor? 46
 3.10 Do Land Surveyors Change Boundaries? 46
 3.11 What is the Cost of Hiring a Land Surveyor? ...47
Chapter 4 Land Surveying and Building 51
 4.1 Building a Fence 52
Chapter 5 Encroachments Easements and Land Conflict 54
 5.1 Encroachment..54
 5.2 Easement 54
 5.3 Land Conflict..54
Chapter 6 Some Misconceptions and Myths Regarding Land Surveying 57
Chapter 7 Property Rights of Spouses 63

Chapter 8   Extract from the Ghana Land Act 2020
            (Act 1036) 68
Chapter 9   Biblical Quotes About Land and Boundaries ...73
Chapter 10   Islamic Religion Landownership 78
Chapter 11   Social Quotes About Land and Boundaries......82
Chapter 12   Some Basic Terminologies in Surveying...........88
Chapter 13   Government Policies and Land
            Administration Reform....................................94
    13.1 National Land Policy Overview 94
    13.2 Institutional Roles in Land
    Administration 101
    13.3 Reform Measures and Their Impact............108
Chapter 14   Community Participation and Awareness 116
    14.1 Community Engagement Strategies 116
    14.2 Public Education Campaigns......................122
    14.3 Empowerment and Capacity Building 127
Chapter 15   Technology and Land Conflict Resolution.....134
    15.1 Digital Land Registries................................134
    15.2 Geographic Information Systems (GIS).......141
    15.3 Mobile and Online Platforms.....................146
Chapter 16   A Holistic Framework for Sustainable
            Land Conflict Resolution 155
    16.1 Integrating Customary and Statutory
    Systems 155
    16.2 Policy and Institutional Coordination.........163

Bibliography... 181
Production Sponsor..185

LIST OF FIGURES

Figure 1: Surveyors on Site xx
Figure 2: African Traditional Rulers 3
Figure 3: State Land and Ghana National Flag 5
Figure 4: An Example of Vested Lands in Ghana 6
Figure 5: Traditional Leaders in Charge of Stool or Skin
           Lands 7
Figure 6: A Piece of Land Owned by a Family 8
Figure 7: Individual Land 9
Figure 9: Land Acquisition Framework in Ghana 10
Figure 10: Land Surveyors Preparing to Measure 23
Figure 11: Professional Surveyor in the Office 25
Figure 12: Land Surveyors at Work 26
Figure 13: Students Understudying a Land Surveyor 27
Figure 14: A Surveyor Ready to Serve 32
Figure 15. Setting Out Exercise by Land Surveyors 52

FOREWORD

Finally, your roadmap for navigating your way through land issues in Ghana and beyond is here! This book, *Ghana Land in Focus Vol. 1*, gets you covered on your land issues. The author, Engr. Surv. Dr. Dr. Ebenezer Ankomah Gyamera, through this book, expounds practically critical land issues, from planning to surveying, documentation, encroachment and conflicts, legal issues, ownership, and development. Through this journey, solutions are provided for effective land and regulation to enhance national development. I got intrigued as I journeyed through this great eye-opening asset, the chronological presentation of useful ideas and solutions to critical challenges within the land sector of today's world. As we plan to acquire and own lands, *Ghana Land in Focus Vol. 1* is a nonnegotiable guide to make our dreams come true.

Take a ride through this book and be sure to come back for a tip and more.

> **PROF. J. S. Y. KUMA**
> **Former Vice Chancellor,**
> **University of Mines and Technology**
> **Tarkwa, Ghana**

Smooth and effective land management is key for national development. This is achievable when all stakeholders possess adequate knowledge on land acquisition, documentation, and development processes. *Ghana Land in Focus Vol. 1* provides useful information on proper land acquisition, documentation, and development process to minimise land conflicts and also ensure proper use of lands. The book highlights on challenges in land management and suggests workable solution procedures for effective land management in Ghana and beyond. As the of director of Lands Commission, I, therefore, recommend this great asset to all stakeholders, including surveyors, lawyers, Land Commission workers, private and public land managers, and clients of all land institutions and companies for our quest for effective land management development.

KWAME TENADU Snr (FGhIS)

**Global Vice President
International Federation of Surveyors (FIG)**

**Past President
Licensed Surveyors Association of Ghana (LiSAG)**

As the traditional leader and a major stakeholder in land acquisition, documentation, development, and land conflict resolution, extensive knowledge on how to effectively undertake land-related responsibilities is a priority. *Ghana Land in Focus Vol. 1* provides insightful and practical enlightenments on the roles and positions of traditional leaders in land management in Ghana. In view of this, *Ghana Lands in Focus Vol. 1* is a recommended treasure for chiefs and other traditional leaders in providing guidance on all related issues at the local traditional level to minimise land disputes for development.

NANA KODWO KONDUA VI
Paramount Chief
Edina Traditional Council
Elmina, Ghana

As a productive engineering company in the land sector, aiding our clients to have a comprehensive knowledge about land acquisition, documentation, and development process is a priority. *Ghana Land in Focus Vol. 1* provides to clients a practical pathway to handling all issues that emerge out of their desire to acquire lands for development. Gyam Engineering and Construction Works Ltd. proudly sponsored the publication of *Ghana Land in Focus Vol. 1* because for the first time, principles and process for land acquisition, documentation, and development is made available to clients for smooth service delivery for national development.

ENGR. MRS. ADWOA A. GYAMERA
Managing Director
Gyam Engineering and Construction Works Ltd.

INTRODUCTION

Land is a gift of nature, and it comprises of components, such as soil, rocks, and natural vegetation. It is also perceived as a communal property that defines a community's geographical extent, as well as its economic strength and sociocultural heritage. Land contains all minerals and holds all buildings and immovable properties. It is regarded as the main pillar for measuring economic growth in terms of capital and wealth. It is a good investment and a valuable asset; it does not depreciate but rather appreciates with time. There is no doubt land is the most important economic asset to humankind. It is hard to visualise any economic activity that does not require the use of land. Interest in land is, therefore, vital in business transactions, an essential prerequisite for any economic venture (Gambrah, 2002). This makes land the most powerful commodity in the world, with high demand rate in all aspects of development.

Land surveying and surveying in general is the measurement and mapping of our surrounding environment using mathematics, specialised technology, and other equipment. Surveying is so important that everybody, directly or indirectly, depends on it to ensure order in the physical world around us. Having your land properly surveyed helps establish property boundaries, an important step for all homeowners and landowners.

Land surveyors play an integral role in land development, from the planning and designing of land subdivisions through to the final construction of any project, such as roads, utilities, and landscaping. A land surveyor measures anything on the land, in the sky, or even on the ocean bed. The surveyor is the first person on any construction site and the last person to leave the site/land. The surveyor works in the office as well as on the field.

Most people have the perception that the sole job of the land surveyor is to measure and map land. This book will, thus, enlighten you on land and the role of a land surveyor in land acquisition, especially in Ghana.

Figure 1: Surveyors on Site

CHAPTER ONE

LAND HOLDINGS AND LAND TENURE SYSTEM IN GHANA

Almost everybody's history or family root is a chronicle of attachment to land or alienation from land (Kolers, 2009). Apart from it being a gift of nature, land is also perceived as a communal property that defines a community's geographical extent, as well as its economic strength and sociocultural heritage.

According to Yongfang and Liangi (2013), land has the following characteristics:

i. **Immobility**: Land cannot be moved from one place to another. It is physically immobile. For example, the supply of serviced lots in one area of a city cannot be increased by additional lots in another part of the city. The forces of demand and supply in real estate markets are determined by the conditions that exist in each local region; transactions in one market area have little impact on transactions in another area. The better the location within the entire community, the higher the value of the land.

ii. **Durability**: Land is physically indestructible and will remain forever; however, obsolescence of use may destroy the land's value or economic durability.

iii. **Uniqueness**: No two parcels of land are ever exactly alike; they differ in at least their geographic locations.

iv. **Scarcity**: Although the physical supply of land is fixed, there is no real shortage of land in total supply.

However, certain types of land in given locations may be in short supply, for example, serviced lots within municipal boundaries or river lots may be scarce.
- *v.* **Rigidity:** Once labour and capital expenditures have been committed for improvements on the land, the investment becomes fixed in place and permanent for all intents and purposes.

1.1 Land Tenure System in Ghana

Ghana has statutory and customary land tenure systems run synchronously together. The customary lands are owned and managed by the traditional societies known as tribes, clans, or families. Article 267 of the Constitution of Ghana (1992) makes it clear that chiefs and family heads are the custodians of such lands and have the authority to enforce right and obligation to the land that has been granted. This system of tenure is applicable to rural, peri-urban, and urban centres. Actually, no land is owned by the state with the exception of the one that has been acquired by lawful proclamation, ordinances, statutory procedures, or international treaties (Kuntu-Mensah, 2006).

1.1.1 Landownership in Ghana

According to Kasanga (1988), there is no land without an owner in Ghana. The owner of a land is, therefore, any person or group of people that have reserved right, legally or customarily, to use, convey, lease, or assign a parcel of land. Land territory, per political philosophy, is the extent to which a landowner's power or right over a particular land end (Avery-Kolers, 2009). Land is vested allodially in the cognate (kinship) group, which includes the living family, together with the ancestors and future generations. This makes landownership joint but not a divided one.

Traditionally, a customary land should not be alienated as it does not belong to the current generation alone. Indigenes claim undeveloped customary lands on behalf of their family units, which over time tends to evolve into family lineage land and then passed on through to family members over generations (Anyidoho *et al.*, 2008). Strangers, migrants outside of the cognate group, may be given the right to live, use, and enjoy portions of the customary land at the pleasure of the customary group. No individual can easily convert his/her status from being a stranger to an indigene. Descendants of migrants who settled on the land some generations back are still considered strangers (Ollenu, 1962). Traditional rulers as displayed in figure 1 are the custodians.

Figure 2: African Traditional Rulers

Basically, there are three main forms of landownership in Ghana: state lands, customary lands, and private lands. However, the current tenure regime in Ghana provides five broad classes of landownership: state lands, vested lands, stool/skin lands, family lands, and individual/private lands.

a) State Lands

These are lands compulsorily acquired by the government for its development functions and are in the absolute ownership of the state. Under the State Land Act 1962 (Act 125), the declaration through the publication of an instrument designating a piece of land as required in the public interest automatically vests ownership of the land in the state. As with expropriation law and policy in many countries, compulsory state land acquisition has to be for development projects deemed to be for the public good. The land can also be acquired in terms of one of the State Property & Contract Act, 1960 (CA 6), and the Land (Statutory Wayleaves) Act 1963 (Act 186). Land may specifically be expropriated under the constitution, in the interest of defense, public safety, public order, public morality, public health, and the development or utilisation to promote the public benefit [Constitution Act 20 of 1962, Article 20(a)].

Every mineral in its natural state in, under, or upon any land in Ghana, rivers, streams, water courses, the exclusive economic zone, and any area covered by the territorial sea or continental shelf is the property of the Republic of Ghana and is vested in the president on behalf of and in trust for the people of Ghana (Article 257 of 1992 Constitution). Displayed below in figure 2 is a state land with a national flag of Ghana.

Figure 3: State Land and Ghana National Flag

b) Vested Lands

An estimated 2% of Ghana's land is vested land (Asiama, 2002). These are lands previously owned by the traditional indigenous community (i.e., town or village) but declared under the Land Administration Act 1962 (Act 123) S7 to be vested in the state and administered for the benefit of the community. Though vested lands are similar to state lands because of the incumbent legal ownership of the state, they do differ. For vested lands, the state possesses the legal interest in the land as a trustee, whilst the indigenous community possesses the beneficial interest as a "beneficiary". Though it removes the power of the customary authority over the land, it does not assume the allodial interest, which remains in the cognate group. The customary authorities are, however, given revenues accruing from the land and the proceeds of every transaction regarding the alienation of the land.

In Ghana, vested lands are mostly found in the Gomoa traditional area, *e.g.*, Winneba, Apam, and Agona Swedru areas. More than 50 % of Ga traditional lands are estimated to be vested lands (Kotey, 2002). The management of these lands is done by the Public and Vested Lands Management Division of the Lands Commission as stipulated in Section 23 under the Lands Commission Act (Act 762).

The problem has to do with the relationship between the Lands Commission and the traditional leaders. In about 85% of cases, the Lands Commission will lease a parcel of the land without informing or making any account to the traditional leaders (Mahama and Dixon, 2006). In view of this, the traditional owners also have to resell the same parcel again to the developer or prevent any development on such land. In other circumstances, the traditional leaders lease the land and the Lands Commission fails to register the document. This has been causing customary land conflict, thereby hindering physical development in such areas. The original idea for which vested lands were created was to avoid land conflicts. But now it is rather creating more conflicts (Asiama, 2002).

No. 27 WINNEBA ROUNDABOUT_9m X 6m VERTICAL_WINNEBA

Figure 4: An Example of Vested Lands in Ghana

c) *Stool or Skin Lands*

This type of land belongs to communities that have a stool or skin as the traditional emblem of the soul of ancestors who originally occupied that parcel of land and, therefore, owned the stool or the skin. The ancestors might have settled there as a result of traversing in search of game (hunting), potable water for fishing, potable water for drinking, fertile land for farming, or running away from war fronts in search of peace. The skin or stool land is administered based on the principles of customary or native law. The occupant of the stool or skin, the chief, administers all the land in trust and on behalf of his people. As a custodian, the chief uses the right attached to the absolute interest to distribute parts or portions of the said land to members of the community, as well as developers who may be strangers. However, according to Clause (3) of Article 267 of the 1992 Constitution of Ghana, any disposition of stool lands must be approved by the Lands Commission and also must conform to the approved development plan of the area concerned. Ghanaians and non-Ghanaians cannot acquire freehold interest to such lands (Asiama, 2002). Chiefs and traditional leaders take charge of stool/skin and family lands as shown in figure 3 below.

Figure 5: Traditional Leaders in Charge of Stool or Skin Lands

d) Family Lands

These lands belong to a particular family, and the absolute interest is operated by the head of that family (*i.e., Abusuapanin*). The family head then uses the usufructuary obligations to the members of the family as well as strangers. Such lands were acquired through conquest, long settlement, or by purchase (Asiama, 2002). Family lands are owned and controlled by family heads as displayed in figure 4 below.

Figure 6: A Piece of Land Owned by a Family

e) Individual/Private lands

When land is acquired by an individual as a private property, it is termed as a private/individual land. Such lands can be inherited or be transferred and are not subject to any family sanctions or restrictions. Holders of such lands are individuals and have freehold right as displayed in figure 5 below.

Figure 7: Individual Land

1.1.2 Land Acquisition in Ghana

Ghana has a good legal framework for land acquisition, but because of lack of transparency on the part of land managers, disputes over lands are numerous. As a result, manifestations of most land conflicts emerge during the process of land acquisition. Figure 1.1 provides a detailed framework for lands acquisition in Ghana.

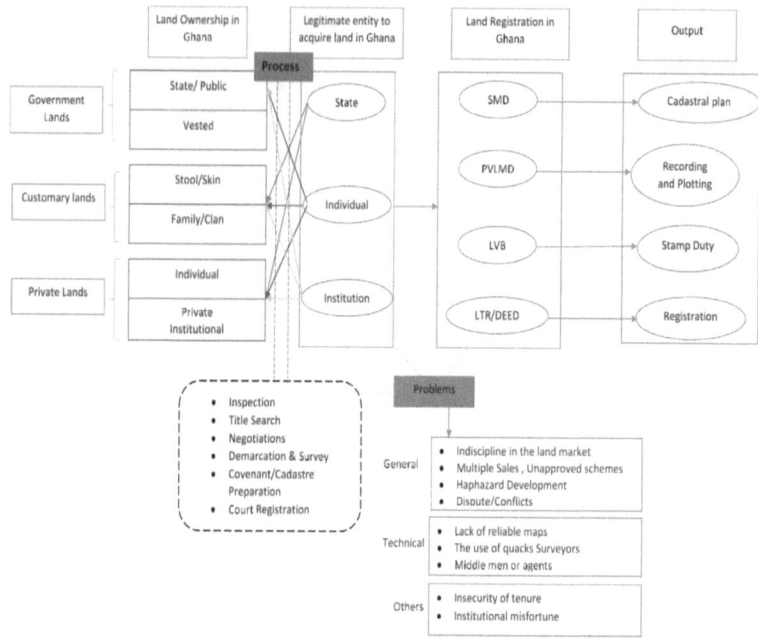

Figure 9: Land Acquisition Framework in Ghana

Land can be acquired in Ghana by citizens and non-citizens of Ghana in any quantity since the constitution does not specify the size of land that can be acquired. Unlike Ghanaian citizens, non-citizens of Ghana are not entitled to freehold interest in any land in Ghana but a lease of not more than 50 years is recommended. However, a citizen of Ghana can acquire lands on freehold interest or leasehold basis for 99 years, subject to renewal for a further term. Land acquired in Ghana can be used for the purpose of residential accommodation, commercial activities, recreation, education, religious activities, agricultural production, etc., depending upon the approved plan/scheme of the area of choice (Kotey, 2002).

Land can be acquired in Ghana from any of the following owners: the state, the stool/skin, the family, and a private person or entity that has title to a particular land (Figure 1.1). It can be acquired by an individual person/entity, any registered group of people, and an institution for any purpose in accordance with the rules and regulations of the state. The following are the procedure in acquiring land in Ghana:

a) Acquiring Land from the Government
Public/state lands are acquired from the government. The process involved in acquiring land from the state can be summarised as follows:

i. Identification of the need and purpose for the land;
ii. Identification of the site of interest in consultations with the Town and Country Planning Office or the Lands Commission;
iii. Securing a site plan that has been prepared in accordance with the development plan of the area. This can be prepared by an official surveyor, a licenced surveyor, or a qualified surveyor confirmed by the director of surveys or the regional surveyor;
iv. Conducting of an official search from the Lands Commission with the development plan or a cadastral plan to know the status of the land;
v. The process is discontinued if the search result is not favourable and look for another land elsewhere;
vi. If the search result is favourable, the process is pursued by submitting an application for government lease containing a declaration of purpose to the executive secretary at the Lands Commission or the regional lands officer, depending on the location of the land. The process is continued at the Lands Commission 'til title to the land is obtained.

vii. Make sure the land is fully registered in your interest before the commencement of any business on the land. Ensure, however, the receipt of all official payments.

It is always advisable to employ the services of a qualified lawyer and land surveyor to guide you through all the processes because of the technicalities involved. Avoid middlemen or agents when acquiring lands. This will minimise conflicts.

b) *Acquiring Land from the Stool/Skin or the Family*
Stool/skin lands or family lands may be acquired from chiefs or family heads, respectively, acting with the consent and concurrence of the elders and senior members of the said stool/skin or family whose consent and concurrence are attested to in the present by some of such elders and senior members as attesting witnesses where the content so requires or admits include his successors in title and assign.

The processes involved are summarised as follows:

i. Identification of the land of interest and the owners;
ii. Identification of the site of interest in consultation with the Town and Country Planning office for its intended purpose and usage;
iii. Securing a cadastral plan of the site. This can be prepared by an official surveyor, a licenced surveyor or a qualified surveyor confirmed by the director of surveys or the regional surveyor;
iv. Obtaining an official search report from the Lands Commission with the cadastral plan to know the status of the land;

v. Confirmation of the ownership of the land from the search report, House of Chiefs, and the surrounding communities;
vi. Discontinue the process if the search result is not favourable and look for another land elsewhere.
vii. If the search result is favourable, the process is continued by negotiating the price and covenants with the owners of the land;
viii. An indenture is drafted containing all the agreements made for proofreading and necessary corrections;
ix. Four copies of the final indenture and a minimum of ten copies of the cadastral plan are then signed by the executers and their witnesses;
x. The documents are taken to court for endorsement;
xi. The next stage is the deed or title registry. This is where deed of title is obtained.
xii. Make sure the land is fully registered in your name before the commencement of any business on the land.

c) *Acquiring Land from Private Owners/Individuals*

Same processes stated above are followed when acquiring a parcel of land from private/individual landowners. However, in this case, the title of the ownership should carefully be inspected to ensure the land is vacant and free from all encumbrances. Validate any site plan provided from the director of surveys, an official surveyor, a licenced surveyor, or any qualified surveyor. Figure 1.1 summarises the framework in acquiring land in Ghana. It is composed of the ownership of lands, the legitimate entity that can acquire the lands, the registration process, and the output of each process. It also accounts for the process in acquiring such lands and the associated problems.

The problems commonly associated with land acquisition in Southern Ghana can be categorised into three: general, technical, and others. The general problems include indiscipline in the land market, multiple sale of lands, the use of unapproved schemes, and haphazard development leading to many conflicts. The technical problems are lack of reliable maps and the use of quack surveyors and middlemen by some clients. Finally, other problems may include insecurity of tenure and institutional misfortune.

1.1.3 Types of Land Agreement or Indenture

1. *Deed of Lease*: This is a simple agreement between owner(s) of land and an individual or organisation interested to rent the land. It can also be a binding contract between a landlord of a commercial property and a prospective tenant outlining the details of the lease. The formal deed of lease is normally prepared in accordance with terms and conditions, like amount of rent, its increment rate, duration of lease, etc. Leases are normally written, signed, and recorded in a registry of deeds.
2. *Deed of Conveyance (freehold)*: This is a signed legal document that shows a title or deed has been transferred. A deed of conveyance is used to prove ownership in a piece of land. It is usually signed, witnessed, and notarised by the seller and the buyer as well as anyone else with a vested interest in the property being transferred.
3. *Deed of Assignment*: This is the agreement between a seller of a portion of a land of property and a buyer of that property showing evidence the seller has indeed transferred all his/her rights, title, interest, and

ownership of that portion of land to the buyer who has just bought the land.

4. *Deed of Gift*: This is a signed document that voluntarily and without remuneration transfers ownership of real, personal, or intellectual property, such as a gift of materials, from one person or institution to another.

1.2 Why People Encounter Problems in Land Acquisition

- They rush.
- They do not listen to expert advice.
- They deal with easily accessible surveyors but unqualified.

1.3 Deed and Title Registration in Ghana

Ghana practices deed registration and title registration, depending upon the region where the land is situated. Out of the total number of 16 political regions of Ghana, the land title registration is practiced in only two regions, namely the Greater Accra Region and Ashanti Region.

1.3.1 Deed Registration

Deed registration is the process of registering all instruments affecting land per the Land Registry Act 1962 (Act 122). Apart from a judge's certificate, the law requires all instruments to be registered and must include a site plan or map containing the description of the land (Cittie, 2006). The purpose of the Land Registry Act was to record the document to the land being registered. Registration of Instrument has been in existence since C18th under Ordinances of the Land Registration

Ordinance, 1883. The Land Registration Ordinance of 1883 was replaced by the Land Registration Ordinance of 1895, which has also been repealed by Land Registry Act 1962 (Act 122).

Deed registration is only helpful in cases of conflict of priority of instrument and does not confer title to land. It is, therefore, for the purpose of evidence of which instrument was registered first (Cittie, 2006). Again, deed registration does not ensure security of title to land to avoid land conflict. Deed registration is, therefore, being challenged by a number of issues, which include inaccurate site plans, multiple sales of lands, insecurity of landownership, thereby leading to several forms of land conflicts.

However, since 2000, deed registration has considerably improved as a result of the introduction of the cadastral plan being the plan attached to the instrument. Cadastral plans are prepared in accordance with the Survey Act 962 (Act 127). The request of the cadastral plan as a fundamental requirement needed for deed registration has considerably reduced fraud in land dealings and the issues of double registration of lands.

A cadastral plan can be defined as a plan showing legal boundaries of individual property. It is a plan prepared to be attached to an instrument for registration purposes. A cadastral plan is prepared by the director of surveys or his/her representative, official surveyor, a licenced surveyor, or any qualified surveyor who is a member of the Ghana Institution of Surveyors.

The cadastral plan has the following essential characteristics amongst others:

i. It is certified and sealed by a licenced surveyor.
ii. It is always approved and sealed by the director of survey or a regional surveyor in the region in which the land is situated.
iii. It contains a regional number and descriptions of the land as plan data.

1.3.2 Title Registration

The land title registration (LTR) was introduced to replace the deed registration by the promulgation of Land Title Registration Law 1986 (PNDCL 152) and the Land Title Regulation 1986 L.I 1241.

LTR had two purposes:

i. To provide certainty and facilitate proof of title to land, and
ii. To create an enabling environment for land transactions. Indications here are to make dealing in land safe, pro-poor, and guarantee security.

Once a land title certificate (LTC) is issued, it becomes indefeasible and can only be revoked by the law court. Laws governing LTR make provision for the registration of all interests held under customary law and common law, which include allodial title, usufruct/customary law freehold, freehold, customary tenancies, and mineral licences (Cittie, 2006). Again, in LTR, the most basic and vital ingredient is the cadastral plan or the parcel plan.

Summary of LTR Process

Application form is obtained from LTR office. The form is filled and summitted by the applicant or the client at the LTR office. Upon submission of the filled application form, the client is issued with an acknowledgement form (yellow card) and a request for parcel plan letter. This letter is to be sent to the Survey Department for the preparation of a parcel plan or cadastral plan of the client's property. After the parcel plan has been prepared, it is sent to the Lands Commission for an official search by the client with a letter from the LTR office. If the search result is favourable, the process is continued by publications in the dailies. If the LTR office does not receive any objections after 21 days from the day of publication, the land title certificate is typed, signed, and recorded on the sectional plans. The client is then called for collection.

1.4 Limitations of Title Registration

The LTR has the following deficiencies:

i. Lack of stakeholder participation
ii. Inadequate archival process
iii. Footprints or details not mandatory
iv. Process not fully automated
v. Conversions of registered deeds to title
vi. Delays in parcel plan preparation and searches
vii. High cost
viii. Objections to publications
ix. Lack of cooperation amongst land agencies

1.5 Challenges in the Land Sector

As noted in the National Land Policy 1999, there are numerous problems and constraints in the land sector. Some are

a. General indiscipline in the land market characterised by the current spate of land encroachments, multiple sale of residential parcels, unapproved development schemes, haphazard development, etc., leading to environmental problems, disputes, conflicts, and endless litigations.
b. Indeterminate boundaries of stool lands as a result of lack of reliable maps/plans and use of unapproved, old, or inaccurate maps and also the use of quack surveyors leading to land conflicts and litigations between stools and other landowning groups.
c. Inadequate security of land tenure because of conflict of interests between and within landowning groups and the state, land racketeering, and weak land administration system.
d. Lack of consultation with landowners and chiefs in decision-making for land allocation, acquisition etc., difficult accessibility of land for agricultural, industrial, and residential purposes because of conflicting claims of ownership etc.
e. Delays in court ruling on land issues. It is estimated that about 57% of the total cases in courts are land cases. The ruling rate is also very slow, 10–20 years, with the likelihood of appeal by the losing party, which can also take some years. Projects are, therefore, halted halfway; some does not even commence at all. Apparently, some litigants grow old whilst others demised whilst having land case in court.

f. Other social problems include the agents (middlemen), identifying the right owners of land, identifying a good land surveyor, getting the right documents (cadastral plan and indenture), getting proper registration of documents, developing the land, emerging conflicts, and land guards. Every day is a free day for macho men and land guards to terrorise innocent investors and developers without any interventions by the law enforcement agencies.
g. The developmental agenda of the state does not take land issues into consideration.
h. Institutions established to administer lands are too weak to implement policies.
i. Fragmented institutional arrangement.
j. Lack, inadequate, and delays in compensation of state-acquired lands.
k. Intermediate land tenure.
l. Delays in processing land documents at the Lands Commission and extortion of monies by some Lands Commission officers from clients.
m. There are no streamline arrangement or policy on land acquisition in Ghana, paving the way for anybody to sell land, which contributes to inconsistencies in land acquisition modus operandi.

1.6 The Way Forward

Recommendations to improve land enterprise are focused on two main directions: first, to the investors and developers, and second, to the government and stakeholders. For future business in the land enterprise, the following are recommended to investors and developers:

i. Beware of hot cake lands.
ii. Don't acquire lands under cover; be very transparent.
iii. It is advisable to acquire land through a professional land surveyor, a lawyer, a valuation officer, or a lands officer.
iv. Be present and witness the signatories of the landowners; take pictures when possible.
v. If the amount is too big, present it under camera.
vi. Avoid agents or middlemen.
vii. Perfect your title deed and inspect all stamps.
viii. Protect your boundaries by planting permanent monuments at the corners or edges of your property.
ix. Alternative dispute resolution (ADR) for land conflict resolution must be used more than the court system.

The following recommendations are directed to the government and stakeholders:

i. Sensitisation of the public on land acquisition in Ghana through the media and role play.
ii. Establishment of fast-track land courts in every regional capital.
iii. Judges must be encouraged to lay heavy sentences on the indecent people in the land enterprise.
iv. Lawyers who defend land tricksters must be punished.
v. Establishment of land guard rapid response unit in the police.
vi. Indentures must include passport-size photographs of the lessor and the lessee.
vii. The government must control land prices in the country.
viii. There must be a participatory policy on urban expansion.

ix. The Lands Commission must be equipped with quality human resource and logistics.
x. The country's land sector needs major reforms and shake ups.

Land acquisition is one of the major contributory factors to the high cost of establishing business in Ghana. Land acquisition can be detrimental or a punishment if proper steps are not followed. The problems in the land sector are as a result of the complexities of ownership and land tenure system in Ghana. The challenges can be dealt with by following the points stated above. The government can also establish an institution purposely to regulate the land market. "Covert emptor", which means "buyer beware", is, therefore, the fundamental rule that can be recommended for all prospective buyers of land in Ghana.

CHAPTER TWO

LAND SURVEYING IN GHANA

After a land has been acquired, it needs to be surveyed, and a land surveyor has a major role to play. Land surveying is the art and science of accurately determining, measuring, and mapping the terrestrial relative positions above, on, or under the surface of the earth. These points are often used to establish land maps and boundaries for ownership or governmental purposes. The American Congress on Surveying and Mapping (ACSM) defines land surveying as the science and art of making all essential measurements to determine the relative position of points and/or physical and cultural details above, on, or beneath the surface of the earth and to depict them in a usable form or to establish the position of points and/or details[1].

Figure 10: Land Surveyors Preparing to Measure

---

[1]

Land surveying is said to be a science as it includes scientific operations, such as gathering of information through observations, measurements in the field, questionnaires, research and data analysis in support of planning, designing, and establishing of boundaries. A person who undertakes such activity is called a *land surveyor*, who may also be called a "professional measurer". The land surveyor deals not only with the mathematical and physical aspects of measuring, but also applies them to the legal aspects of boundary law. He/she is responsible for officially marking land boundaries for all construction projects and legal deeds or titles.

2.1 Surveying and Technology

Technology has come to affect how land surveyors work. Introduction of modern instruments, such as global positioning system (GPS), used to measure the land has now reduced the physical labour involved in measuring and has come to increase the accuracy as compared with the traditional way of measuring and application of mathematics to work, thereby increasing the speed of work and reduction of errors.

2.1.1 Who Is a Professional Surveyor?

A professional land surveyor has been qualified by education and experience and has passed an examination for registration required by the laws of the state in which he/she is practising. A professional surveyor is licenced by the state.

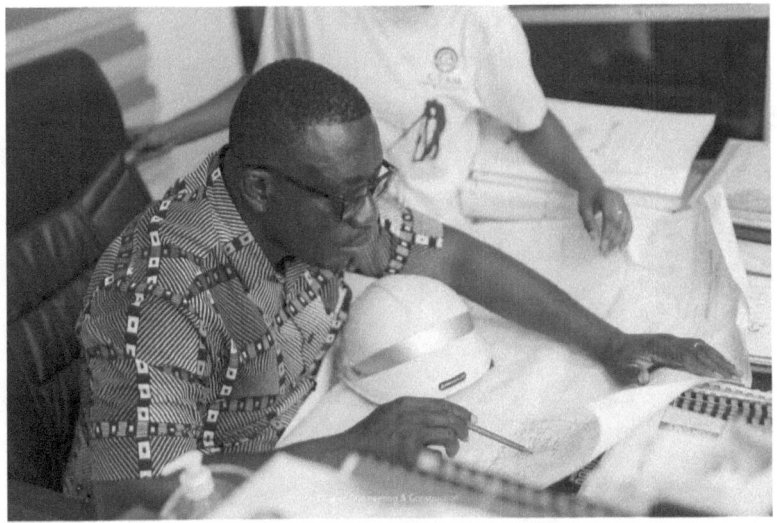

Figure 11: Professional Surveyor in the Office

2.1.2 The Difference amongst Licenced, Registered, or Professional Surveyor

There are no differences amongst licenced, registered, or professional surveyor. Differing terminologies could be used to refer to a land surveyor. However, these terminologies used can be summed up with these abbreviations: RLS (registered land surveyor), LS (land surveyor), PS (professional surveyor), or a PLS (professional land surveyor).

2.1.3 The Work of a Land Surveyor

A land surveyor performs a variety of vital tasks, such as boundary surveys, topographic mapping, and construction staking. Before roads, railways, reservoir, dams, retaining walls, bridges, or residential areas are built, the services of a surveyor is needed. He/she helps establish the boundaries of legal descriptions and the boundaries of various lines of political divisions. A land surveyor, as well, creates maps and plans for the development of property as he/she provides advice and data for *geographic information systems* (GIS). GIS, however, is a computer database that contains data on land features and boundaries.

Figure 12: Land Surveyors at Work

2.1.4 Careers in the Profession of Land Surveying

Students and others understudying surveying sometimes seem not to know their fate in the world of business, making most land surveyors do it simply because they enjoy it. However, in these recent days, this quality of job satisfaction is increasingly gaining more and more importance in our world, making the demand for it great. Many people enjoy land surveying because it is a job with a lot of variety that can offer work in the outdoors and which also involves the ability to think fast and wisely.

Figure 13: Students Understudying a Land Surveyor

What is, therefore, the secret behind this? There are many reasons for land surveyors to have gone through the road to professional licensure. One biggest reason is the enhanced career potential enjoyed by licenced professionals. In spite of various people granted to practice exemption from licensure, these exemptions vary amongst jurisdictions, and there is no guarantee these exemptions are permanent. In fact, many jurisdictions are actively working to eliminate some exemptions. Licensure as a professional land surveyor is a sign of commitment to your profession.

2.1.5 Practising Cadastral Land Surveying in Ghana

Per the 1992 constitution of the country, only the director of surveys and licenced surveyors are mandated to conduct cadastral surveys in Ghana. However, any qualified professional surveyor who wants to practice cadastral surveys may do so only under the supervision of a licenced surveyor of good standing.

In addition, that professional land surveyor must be a member of Ghana Institution of Surveyors (GhIS). Licensure is one of the requirements needed to become a professional land surveyor in Ghana and her territories. Licences are normally issued by the sector minister through the director of surveys to the qualified and deserving land surveyors. Being a licenced land surveyor means you have qualified by education and gained experience in addition to passing examinations required by the laws of the state or country of licensure. An individual accorded the title "licenced surveyor" has to be confirmed with the State Board of Registration.

2.1.6 Practising Surveying without a Licence

The exact definition changes from state to state. However, a portion of Minnesota State Law defines practising surveying as *any person, who offers to perform, holds themselves out as able to perform, or who does perform Land surveying for others, shall be practising land surveying.*[2]

In Ghana, a person is said to be practising surveying without a licence if the person has attended Kwame Nkrumah University of Science and Technology (KNUST)-Kumasi, the University of Mines and Technology (UMaT)-Tarkwa, or the Survey School of Ghana, Accra, and has passed all examination in land surveying. He/she must also have a practical knowledge and experience in the fieldwork in addition to the school certificate. That surveyor must also work under a licenced surveyor for an unspecified number of years.

---

[2] Anon 2016

2.1.7 Having a Complaint about a Land Surveyor

It is always wise and necessary to talk to the land surveyor about your concerns and ask them to explain further when you don't understand anything he/she is doing. Though it is rare any action is necessary, there are few things to remember when you encounter any problem with a land surveyor. Remember, communication is of great importance in any disagreement.

Be sure you have all the fees and understand the scope of work defined by the contract before any work proceeds so you can avoid any future problems.

Many states have state surveyors associations and societies, which have a complaint committee that acts as a mediator to assist the client who has disagreements or misunderstanding(s) with a land surveyor. In Ghana, you can consult the Ghana Institution of Surveyors (GhIS) or Licensed Surveyors Association of Ghana after you have asked the land surveyor and still found no satisfaction to your complaint. Ghana Institution of Surveyors (GhIS), for instance, is the leading source of professional advice on landed property and construction in Ghana.

2.2 How Land Survey Affects Human Life

Surveying has been an essential element in the development of the human environment since the beginning of recorded history, (about 5,000 years ago. Surveyors, therefore, deal with a lot of important issues in our lives, but the three that seem most timeless and universal are our families, our health, and our rights to our land. Our welfare is directly affected by our ability to define our space, which is one of the land surveyor's most important jobs: to mark, describe, and map landownership. The land surveyor works to create a stable framework on which we can build our homes and communities as well as the creation of the wealth necessary to sustain those communities. It is important to admit that knowing the boundaries of our land is an essential part of human life. This is because we cannot enjoy any unique use of life if we do not know the location of the boundaries of our land. To enhance an effective selling, buying, mortgaging, or developing a land in an orderly and predictable fashion, it is advisable that a land surveyor be consulted.

Surveying can be practiced as private or under the Public Land Survey System, which has its own rules. Though the rules may vary depending on where it is practised, there's one fundamental principle that governs the work, and this can be found in the words of Justice Cooley of the Michigan Supreme Court: *"No man loses title to his land or any part of it merely because the evidence of where it once was becomes uncertain."*[3] It could be deduced the perpetuation of property rights and title is tied to the land.

In their activities, land surveyors use computers, precise measuring tools, and mapping systems to collect and analyse data in the field. They then interpret the data to establish the most probable location for property corners. Usually, their opinions made are influenced by the knowledge of common law, rules of evidence, state and federal laws, and local standards of practice.

Despite the fact there are a lot of modern tools available now to make expert measurers out of novices, one will never really know

---

[3]

the true location of boundary lines if we do not understand the value of what is being measured, and that is the expertise of the land surveyor and the reasons why one may see someone carrying a red and white pole with something that looks like a Frisbee on top of it peeking under the sod in your front yard (*William P. Brown, L. S. (MN), Communicator, July 2004 (Publication of AELSLAGID)*).

CHAPTER THREE
THE NEED OF A SURVEYOR

A land surveyor offers a highly technical and complex service often little understood by the general public. As already stated, surveying has been an essential element in the development of the human environment since the beginning of recorded history, about 5,000 years ago, and it is the basic requirement in the planning and execution of nearly every form of construction. It is mostly familiar in the fields of transport, building and construction, communications, mapping, and the definition of legal boundaries for landownership. The land surveyor is often a member of a professional team, who works closely with the state attorney, title company, architect, civil engineer, and others. The land surveyor is often the first on the property, preparing the foundation upon which a project is to be built, and the last to leave.

Figure 14: A Surveyor Ready to Serve

3.1 Some Departments and Agencies Land Surveyors Work For

Some of the departments and agencies land surveyors work for include

1. Attorneys
2. Departments of public works
3. Businesses and companies
4. Energy and utility companies
5. Title insurance companies
6. Bureau of Land Management
7. Ghana Forest Service
8. Department of Agriculture
9. Geographic information system (GIS) departments
10. Department of Fish and Wildlife
11. Banks and other lending institutions
12. Ghana Geological Survey
13. Construction firms
14. Private landowners
15. Government agencies
16. Engineering firms
17. Homeowners and landowners
18. National Geodetic Survey
19. Land developers
20. Departments of transportation
21. Real estate developers
22. Photogrammetrists, etc.

In effect, everybody needs a land surveyor in one way or another. The land surveyor can even serve as an expert witness in court or representative of a client at planning, commission meetings, or other public hearings when local government approval is required for certain projects. The possession of a licence enables the land surveyor to assume such responsibility for the accuracy and precision of the boundary determination.

3.2 Types of Land Surveys

It is necessary for you to know the type of surveying needed from your land surveyor. Having the knowledge of it helps you in giving out adequate and required information to the land surveyor. Below are some types of surveying:

1. Boundary Survey

A boundary survey establishes the true property corners and property lines of a parcel of land. Boundary surveys are typically performed to obtain building permits, to resolve property disputes, and for erecting fences. Easement lines may also be located, if requested, with this type of survey.

2. Cadastral Survey

The cadastral survey has to do with the legal survey, resurvey, or retracement of public lands within the Public Land Survey System of the country for restoration of property lines. Simply put, it is a systematic recording of legal boundaries of a property.

3. Construction Survey

Survey measurements made prior to or whilst construction is in progress to control elevation, horizontal position, dimensions, and configuration, i.e., stakeout of line and grade for buildings, fences, roads, etc.

4. Control Survey

This is a land survey providing precise locations of horizontal and vertical positions of points for use in boundary determination, mapping for aerial photographs, construction-staking, or other needs.

5. Court Exhibit or Judicial Survey

It is the analysis of various legal descriptions and survey maps, field locating of records, existing monuments, physical features, and mapping showing this information for the purpose of presenting a visual exhibit to be used in a courtroom. In some areas in the United States, this may also be known as a "Torrens" Survey of "Registered" or "Torrens" land. A "judicial" survey is a land survey ordered by the courts system, at times setting judicial land marks (JLMs). Some also may refer to these as judicial monuments or judicial markers (JMs).

6. Elevation or Floodplain Survey

Elevation surveys determine the elevation of various sections of a building or land. Typically, these are used to aid in building plans and to determine if a property is in a flood zone.

7. Geodetic Survey

This is a land survey affected by and takes into account the curvature of the earth and astronomic observations.

8. GIS and LIS Surveying and Mapping

This has to do with surveying land using geographic information systems (GIS) and land information systems (LIS).

9. Hydrographic and Underwater Surveys

It is the collecting of data relating to bodies of water and may include the water depth, bottom contours and configuration, directions and velocity of current, heights and water stages, and the location of fixed objects for navigational purposes.

10. Lot Split Survey

Lot split survey is needed when you may need to divide an existing parcel of land into two or more. All surveys for lot splits include a plat of the new parcels and the required legal description to record the split. It is important to note the size of the original parcel as well as the size of the proposed new parcel(s) in the comments section of the request form in to receive accurate quotes.

11. Lot Survey (Site Plan Survey or Plot Plan Survey)

It is a combination of boundary and topographic surveys for preparation of a site plan to be used for designing improvements or developments and obtaining government building permits.

12. Mining and Other Subsurface Surveys

These are surveys that determine the location and dimensions of underground parts of a mine, including the natural and artificial features of the mine, above and below ground. Such surveys are done with vertical and horizontal controls, locating the features in a three-dimensional manner.

13. Mortgage Inspections

Mortgage inspections are not necessarily a land survey, but they are used for consistent purposes in all states. They are often a product provided on residential loans. A drawing may or may not be provided. Be aware many of these "mortgage inspection" surveys are *not boundary surveys*. Often they are required by lending institutions. Fences and other improvements should not be constructed based on a mortgage inspection. This is because boundary lines are not determined on many "mortgage inspection" surveys. It is necessary to look for the "certification" of the land surveyor, which usually includes the signature with the land surveyor's licence number and state of practice.

14. Mortgage Location Survey (Not Necessarily a Land Survey)

These surveys are typically used by title companies and mortgage lenders to obtain proof that the major improvements on the property are free of encroachments onto neighboring properties or into recorded easements. Mortgage surveys do not establish property corners or property lines and may not be used for building purposes.

15. Quantity Surveys

A quantity surveyor obtains measurements of quantities, usually in conjunction with a construction process, earthwork, etc. Oftentimes the quantity surveyor works closely with a civil engineer, architect, or landscape architect.

16. Record or As-Built Survey

It is a survey performed to obtain horizontal and/or vertical dimensional data so a constructed facility may be delineated, i.e., foundation survey or as-built of improvements. Specifically, an as-built survey is to physically locate structures and improvements on a parcel of land, generally for mortgage purposes. This does not always include boundary monumentation.

17. Registered Land Survey (RLS)

A survey of "registered" (Torrens title) land is usually done to shorten lengthy legal descriptions or divide larger parcels of "Torrens title" land into smaller tracts.

18. Route Survey

Route survey is a reconnaissance, preliminary survey and location survey for an alignment or linear-type feature, such as a road, railroad, canal, pipeline, or utility line.

19. Subdivision Survey

Subdivision survey, also known as a subdivision plat, is the subdivision of a tract of land into smaller parcels, showing monumentation and mathematical survey data on a map, conforming to local government, usually county, ordinances.

20. Topographic Survey

It has to do with a land survey locating natural and man-made features, such as buildings, improvements, fences, elevations, land contours, trees, streams, etc. This type of survey may be required by a government agency or may be used by engineers and/or architects for the design of improvements or developments on a site.

21. ALTA Survey or Extended Title Insurance Coverage Survey

A survey made for the purpose of supplying a title company and lender with survey and location data necessary for the issuing of title and/or mortgage insurance. A detailed map is required to be done to the specifications of American Land Title Association (ALTA). Specifications of this type of survey include, but are not limited to, determining property lines, location of improvements, identifying all easements, utilities, and other conditions affecting the property.

ALTA surveys are very comprehensive and typically cost thousands of dollars and take weeks to complete. Any ALTA land survey must meet the "minimum standard detail requirements for ALTA/ACSM land title surveys" as adopted by the American Land Title Association, the American Congress on Surveying and Mapping, and the National Society of Professional Surveyors. The ALTA survey is most often performed on commercial properties.

3.3 Why and When Would I Need a Land Surveyor?

The wish of many land buyers is to know where the boundary lines are. They become more eager to know more about the land before they even finalise the purchase of the property. Below are reasons that may give you some more ideas about why and when you would benefit from a land survey:

1) When you don't know clearly the boundary line of the land you are purchasing or selling.
2) When the land is not clearly defined by a plat, legal description, or older land survey.
3) When you are not convinced with the location of your property corners.
4) To determine drainage, setbacks, and proper planning when building a house, fence, shed, or anything closer to an unknown property line to avoid settlement problems.
5) When dividing land.
6) Most often lending and other financial institutions require a survey for a mortgage.

7) In some situations, an attorney, bank, or title insurance requires a land surveyor to clear up any ambiguous land description or verify the location of structures on the property to finalise a loan grant.
8) When cutting timber near a property line.
9) Usually, in the purchase of title insurance, surveying is needed.
10) It is one of the prerequisites when applying to register your land title.
11) Whenever a boundary line is not known or is in dispute.
12) When settling land disputes.
13) When you think you might have encroached or another person might have encroached on your land.
14) Before developing or establishing property.
15) When building a fence.
16) When erecting a signboard.
17) During construction of buildings and pavement.

3.4 What a Land Surveyor Could Do for You

A common misconception about a land surveyor is they only work with builders. In reality, land surveyors work with a variety of stakeholders, including individuals, government agencies, title companies, real estate professionals, and more. There are many things a land surveyor can do for you:

1) A land surveyor serves as consultant or advisor on whether you need a land survey and the type of land survey to suit your interests: building, developing, or settling legal boundary issues.
2) He/she finds or replaces and marks property corners and lines for easy boundary identification.

3) A surveyor helps create subdivision "plats". A *plat* is an officially drawn map of a land area that defines the boundaries between different parcels of property to scale.
4) In request for elevations, the land surveyor draws topographical and contour maps for drainage and other planning needs.
5) The surveyor advises and cooperates with your attorney, title insurer, realtor, banker, architect, or civil engineer.
6) In locating encroachments and improvements, such as buildings, fences, etc., relative to the property line, the services of a land surveyor are needed.
7) A land surveyor may appear in court as an expert witness on your behalf in court proceedings.
8) In preparing drawings for proposed construction for building permit applications, the land surveyor may assist in such drawings.
9) The land surveyor performs preliminary route surveys for roads and engineering designs. He, as well, performs construction-staking from engineering or architectural design plans.
10) He/she assists in creating a "basemap" to develop geographic information system (GIS).
11) In the work of a land surveyor, latitude and longitude of features or control points are accurately defined using specified coordinate systems or datum, usually global positioning system (GPS).

3.4.1 What You Should Know or Ask When Hiring a Land Surveyor

Here are some tips that will help yourself and the land surveyor:

- You must have enough information about the surveyor before awarding the surveying contract.

- When contacting a land surveyor, you need to visit his/her business premises but not the house.
- As much as possible, allow enough time. Surveying involves researching and planning, and your job has to fit into the workload of the land surveyor.
- Other land surveyors might have worked before in the area where your property is being surveyed. Ask if they have worked in your area, surveyed your property or that of your neighbors. Usually, it is cost effective when land surveyors are familiar with the area in question.
- The experience and expertise of the land surveyor matters a lot. Ask the surveyors of the experience they have in performing the type of survey you are requesting. You may ask the land surveyor to show you proof that he/she is a registered professional land surveyor.
- You may have your time schedules at which you want the project to be completed; ask if he/she will be able to complete the land survey within the time frame you require.
- Ask if his /her service is charged per hour or per job. Do not forget to ask when you have to pay the cost involved.
- Ask if the property lines and corners in the field would be shown to you and how you could find the property lines from now onward on the basis of the land survey. Don't mistake traverse lines for your property lines.
- Ask the land surveyor any questions bothering your mind. It is mandatory for them to provide you with answers to any question in the matter being presented or discussed. This is one of the reasons you hired the service of the land surveyor.
- Inspect your property lines regularly. This is to protect your property corners from destruction or encroachment

by others. Take note: Never relocate property corners for any reason.
- Do not seek the cheapest services of a land surveyor. In contracting a land surveyor, you must look for one who will do the most satisfactory job for you.

3.5 Information You Should Supply the Land Surveyor

Mostly time is much spent verifying the correctness of property corners or points of beginning than is spent in setting property corners. For efficiency and effectiveness, you must furnish the land surveyor with much information prior to the fieldwork. This, in the end, may also help reduce your costs. Supply information even if you might think it would negatively affect your boundaries.

It is important to understand that although you may only want your own property lines surveyed, the land surveyor is also determining the boundary of the neighbor's land and must be impartial in the location of any boundary line. There is much information you may give to the land surveyor. Here are some of the facts you may supply the land surveyor to aid his/her work:

1) Explain to the land surveyor the exact purpose of the survey; thus, define your needs. Based on that, the land surveyor may often suggest ideas you have not thought of.
2) Never forget to ask questions if you do not seem to understand what is being presented or discussed.
3) Supply "proof of ownership", such as legal description of the property, like the lot, block, subdivision name, aliquot part description, a copy of a title opinion, title

search, title insurance, and other documents. These documents should be genuine and from a reliable source.
4) Readily provide any additional old surveys, plats, plot plans, or building plans and indentures.
5) Make known all disputes over the property or its corners or boundaries.
6) Make known any information you may have about your property and its location of the property lines or corners.
7) Provide information about adjoining landowners.

3.6 What Does the Land Surveyor Do When You Hire Him/Her?

Depending upon the circumstances, the work of a land surveyor is likely to include the following:

1) He/she locates and describes land or property boundaries on the ground. Usually, the surveyor's opinion about your land is based on his/her knowledge on title opinion, title certificate, and certificate of title, deed, or other form of "proof of ownership".
2) The surveyor does research on the available records of your property and often adjoining properties for any possible conflicts. The land surveyor then takes measurements of the property lines to identify and justify your property lines based on the data gathered from the research. This may take much time and several trips to the property site. The boundary of the property is determined after the measurement and the data are analysed. The land surveyor may then make known any evidence of encroachments or defects on your

property and give a professional opinion as to where the boundaries of the property are.
3) The land surveyor finds and confirms the accuracy of your property lines and/or replaces them when necessary. Having additional "points set on the property line" is helpful as these points might be used for other purposes, such as fencing, construction in hilly terrain, on lines which have their end of the line in water, or along long property lines. Make known to the land surveyor if you find it beneficial to have additional "points set online" before the work begins. In doing this, the land surveyor may survey property adjacent to yours to confirm the accuracy of your property lines. Do not, therefore, be surprised if you find the land surveyor working in your neighborhood in addition to your property.
4) The land surveyor also advises you of any legal matters involved in the land survey or legal problems encountered during the land survey, referring you to an attorney if needed.

3.7 What Do You Get from a Land Surveyor?

What a land surveyor can do for you may vary from one location to another and the local requirements. The need of the client, contractor, architect, engineer, or any other person working with the land surveyor may determine the surveyor's work.

3.8 Should the Land Surveyor Tell You What You Own?

The land surveyor works best when you provide him/her with enough information about the property called "proof of ownership" as the land surveyor describes, interprets, and compares your proof of ownership to field evidence of ownership. These may include legal description, current title opinion, or title policy concerning the parcel you want to survey. The surveyor then locates the property on the ground, marks corners with physical monuments, and provides record of the land survey showing the results. Areas in conflict could, therefore, be disclosed by the surveyor so agencies, such as title company and attorney, can resolve any problem.

3.9 Will You Be Shown Your Property Corners and Lines by the Surveyor?

It is reasonable to know where your property lines and corners are located. However, property corners are usually found or replaced by the land surveyor. The surveyor usually shows this on the client's request. Usually, the monument marked for the property corner set is identified with regional numbers of the region. These property corners are mostly set beneath the earth surface for durability and permanence.

3.10 Do Land Surveyors Change Boundaries?

It must be emphasised land surveyors cannot and do not take away land or give away land to anyone on any grounds. Conflict is bound to happen sometimes when the recorded description, which is based on legal records, do not agree with the way the property has actually been occupied.

The land surveyor, therefore, establishes these property lines according to the legal recorded land descriptions, and in so doing, some lines may depart from occupation and give the appearance of change initiated by the land surveyor. Nonetheless, the land surveyor does not just mark the land out but follows the footsteps of the original land survey. The land surveyor, therefore, replaces corners where evidence has shown they were originally set.

3.11 What is the Cost of Hiring a Land Surveyor?

Surveying involves a process, from research of records to examination of physical evidence of prior surveys. Therefore, the total cost of hiring the services of a land surveyor cannot be quantified as the cost of a land survey is directly proportional to the total effort and time used. Basically, in giving you an estimated proposal for his/her service, the land surveyor estimates the cost for you based on some determinants, such as

(1) ***Availability of Information and Records***
This is one of the factors that can affect the amount to be paid to your land surveyor. Making past transactions on the land may or may not affect the cost charge. Sometimes land transactions may have been handled poorly in the past, resulting in vague, incomplete, and often contradictory legal descriptions and deeds. This may need extra work to be done by the land surveyor, and this may as well attract an additional cost.

(2) ***Accessibility***
Familiarity with the area of survey to the land surveyor may also mean he/she might have readily available records of that land and its neighborhood. Time to perform the fieldwork is, more often than not, determined by the

distance to and the difficulty in reaching the property corners necessary to complete the work.

(3) ***Presence and Evidence of Survey Monuments***
A land surveyor works effectively when there are reorganised land monuments, such as survey pillars/beacons, iron/wood/stone monuments, old fences or occupation lines, witness trees, and parole evidence (i.e., oral evidence). Someone pointing out accepted occupation lines and monuments can be an effective aid to the land surveyor, especially prior to the fieldwork. Absence of these may increase the difficulty in retracing the original survey, which may also attract a high cost.

(4) ***Complexity, Sectionalised Land (PLS-Rectangular Survey System)***
Whenever a land is described in this manner, it may require a survey of the entire section (i.e., one square mile) in which the land being surveyed lies, regardless of the location the parcel itself lies. However, a survey of more than one section may be required but is mostly determined by the location of the land parcel and availability of government (PLS) monuments.

5) ***Improvements (Houses, Garages, Fences, Pavement, Etc.)***
If improvement locations, such as a house, fence, garage, etc., are required to be located, there is the need for additional measurements on the fieldwork. It is usually advised that improvements are to be located and placed on the certificate of survey for referencing. It is recommended that your house or garage be "tied into" your property line, which will show the distances from

the building corners to your property line. This will, in the end, allow you to easily locate your property line near your buildings or other improvements.

(6) **Equipment Required to Perform the Job**
Any specialised equipment involved in the surveying could increase the cost of the project. The type of survey may influence the choice of an instrument to be used. The use of drones and Real Time Kinematic (RTK) may increase the cost of the project.

(7) **Size of the Parcel**
The size and the shape of the land parcel may or may not influence the cost. For example, an irregularly shaped parcel has more corners to pick than a rectangular parcel containing the same area. It should be noted, however, there is no special relationship factor between the size of the parcel and the cost of the land survey. Many people, more often than not, incorrectly equate a "small lot" with a "small price" of the land survey and a "large parcel" with a "larger or more expensive" price, but it is not always like that.

(8) **Time of Year and Weather Conditions**
Weather conditions largely determine the cost of a land survey project. For example, foggy weather hinders accessibility to the site as well as making it more difficult to work on the site. Rainy season may sometimes hide field evidence as well.

(9) **Topography, Terrain, and Vegetation**
The shape or topography of the parcel of the land may or may not make the project difficult, which will, in

effect, also affect the cost involved. A level parcel of land, for example, is easier to survey than a land found on a mountainous area. Before going to the field, land surveyors usually ask if the work will involve clearing a line, brush branches, and small trees in the field, which may possibly affect a line of sight for the fieldwork. However, shrubs, flowers, and trees on home sites, normally, do not disturb fieldwork but might need additional time to work around them.

(10) *Type of Land Survey Required*

As mentioned earlier, there are many types of land survey. ALTA land surveys and title company requirements, for example, may require more documentation and fieldwork than is normally required by the average property owner. Therefore, costs may increase should the required precision and extent of the land survey increase.

CHAPTER FOUR

LAND SURVEYING AND BUILDING

In most situations, land survey is one of the requisites in obtaining a permit to build. This will enable you to know and protect your investment; thus, you would be building on your own property. This has been a problem since ages, when some people build on a land they claim to be their property, yet it is legally not. It must be emphasised the location of any existing structures may be helpful as new improvements are significant to prepare a topographic map, which may help determine a finished floor elevation, which will allow for drainage and a pleasing appearance.

A construction (building) plan is made, after which a land surveyor can stake the proposed building corners and transfer them accurately to the ground and to the final construction. There is the need for a construction plan to help you meet setback requirements and other limitations enforced by any local government agency. Avoiding this could make you lose a future sale if the purchasers have an up-to-date survey done. Mortgage lenders usually do not advance money until zoning law infringements are cleared up.

Figure 15. Setting Out Exercise by Land Surveyors

4.1 Building a Fence

You may ask, "Do I need a land surveyor when building a fence or wall?" This varies from one country to another. Nevertheless, there are requirements you must meet before constructing a fence or wall. In Ghana, for instance, you need to consult the Surveying and Mapping Division of the Lands Commission or Building Inspectorate Division before you can construct a fence or wall. Whatever the case may be, it is reasonable to validate your property lines before the construction. Besides, when you employ a land surveyor, the pros and cons of the location of your fence can be known. Having a land surveyor work with you also ensures the construction of the fence does not remove your property corners.

How Close to the Property Line Can You Build Your Fence?

Usually, there is confusion in this area on what to do. Some people believe they have the right to build right on the property line. However, this ideology has its own setback. Some questions you must ask before proceeding with the erection of the fence/wall include

- ✓ Does it encroach over the property line?
- ✓ Will you have to use your neighbour's property to paint or stain your new fence?
- ✓ How do you maintain the other side of the fence?
- ✓ What about the size of the footings for the fence posts?

To avoid all these questions and their troubles, you are entreated to consult the Surveying and Mapping Division of the Lands Commission, the building inspectorate, or a private surveyor for any requirements about your fencing. These agencies will show you if there are any requirements to satisfy your location, height requirements, and land survey because there are many misconceptions about general rules of fencing, which are only hearsay or rumours.

CHAPTER FIVE

ENCROACHMENTS EASEMENTS AND LAND CONFLICT

5.1 Encroachment

Encroachment is an act where a person intrudes or trespasses upon an improvement, a building, or other property of another. This is the act of trespassing.

5.2 Easement

Easement is the right to use the real property of another for a particular purpose. Easement itself is a real property interest, but legal title to the underlying land is retained by the original owner for all other property. Easements can take different forms, either permanent or temporary, surface easements, subsurface easements, or overhead easements.

5.3 Land Conflict

Land conflict can be defined as a social fact in which at least two parties are involved, the roots of which are different interests over the property rights to land: the right to use the land, to manage the land, to generate an income from the land, to exclude others from the land, to transfer it, and the right to compensation for it. However, if the social positions of the parties involved differ greatly, a land conflict can be understood as a misuse, restriction, or dispute over property rights to land (Wehrmann 2005).

Much detail about land conflict has been explained in *Ghana Land in Focus Vol. 2*.

Can Surveying Determine If Your Property Is Encroached Upon?

This can only be done at your request to the land surveyor to show any encroachment onto your property, as well as if you are or may be encroaching upon your neighbor's property.

Will Easements Be Shown on Your Property?

Easements may usually appear on the land survey drawing. To facilitate this, the landowner normally provides a current title report, title opinion, certificate of title, or title policy to use for this purpose.

Does Title Insurance Prevent Boundary Problems?

Title insurance, as it is, protects the lending institution as well as the property owner, if insured, against claims to the property that cause a disputed boundary. This is guided by a policy called *lender's policy*, where it is required of the home buyer by mortgage lenders to purchase a title insurance policy in the lender's name. Many people do not know of *survey exception*, which explains that title insurance policies do not give coverage against encroachments, easements, and boundary disputes that could be disclosed by a current certified survey. There is also the need to know that many people do not know that if you want to cover yourself, you need to pay an additional charge. There is a relationship between the survey exception and survey endorsement as mortgage lenders routinely require a survey endorsement to their loan policies that limits the scope of the survey exception to the specific problems disclosed on a survey. It is always required and advised that homebuyers insist on an owner's title insurance policy with a survey endorsement based on a current land survey system.

CHAPTER SIX

SOME MISCONCEPTIONS AND MYTHS REGARDING LAND SURVEYING

1. **The Difference between a New Surveyed Land and Other Older Surveyed Land**

You may ask, "Why is my new land survey different from another older land survey?" The answer lies in the definition of land surveying; it is an art and science of accurately determining, measuring, and mapping the terrestrial relative positions above, on, or under the surface of the earth. Therefore, discrepancies between surveys are usually attributable to two reasons: First, measurements are bound to error; thus, two conducted measurements on the same line may give different results. Though both measurements may be close, they may only approach the true value through precision, repetition, and statistical analysis. Second, measurements are made from or with the decisions based on found evidence. It will surprise you to know that surveys done at different times may not have the same evidence available. Thus, recent survey, for example, may have the benefit of monuments set after the prior survey, whereas previously existing monuments used for the prior survey may or may not be available. There is another source of evidence, which may be reliable, and that is the records that the land surveyor has in his/her possession. This may include years and years of *field notes* and original *certificates of survey*, which always remain the property of the land surveyor.

2. The Government Surveyor and Private Land Surveyor

The most common question people ask is, "What does a government surveyor do?" Can't he survey a land? Simply, government surveyors barely survey private property. Landowners are usually referred to private land surveyors for their services. The duties and responsibilities of a government surveyor is always best explained and detailed by the local county surveyor. However, government surveyor's offices serve the public with the following services:

- Re-monumentation and maintenance of the public land survey monuments within the area.
- Restoring any lost or obliterated public land survey monuments.
- Maintaining land surveying files and creating highway right-of-way maps.
- Performing global positioning (GPS) control surveys for a basis of control for others.
- Producing land surveys for other county departments as needed.
- Reviewing certified land surveys, registered land surveys, and subdivision plats, checking compliance with state and local laws.
- Helping answer the public and other institutions with bothering land surveying-related questions.

Considering the above responsibilities of a county surveyor, some local government authorities have recognised the benefits of having a full-time county surveyor on staff.

3. Unusual Encroachment over a Property Line

In surveying land, surveyors usually make out encroachments. This makes the assertion that a land survey is a good investment in a property line.

4. Title Insurance Guarantees Your Property against All Encroachment Problems

No, title insurance does not cover encroachments, easements, and boundary line disputes, which are only disclosed by a current land survey.

5. Every City or Government Agency Has a Land Surveyor

This is just a misconception; however, there is truth in it, as many organisations do, whilst others do not. Some agencies will also seem as if they have a licenced land surveyor on staff.

6. All Land Is Already Surveyed; I Just Have to Find the Survey.

This usually happens when people who lived in a place before are believed to have surveyed the land. It may be true that all land may be identified and often mapped for tax purposes, but usually, the previous survey may not always help you in gathering data on the ground.

7. Next Door to Me, They Are Building. They Must Have Had a Land Survey.

Not necessarily the case may be true. It is proper to check from the local government authorities, and if necessary, ask the people concerned about it. In Ghana, you need to consult or check from the building inspectorate. This will, in the long, run help as it is a good idea for landowners to know where their property lines or corners are.

8. People Can Possess Land Using "Adverse Possession"

This is, more often than, not talked about, but it is very difficult to prove. Consult your land surveyor and attorney.

9. A Friend of Mine Can Identify My Property Corner or Property Line for Me

It is advisable to get your land surveyed by a licenced land surveyor. This is so based on two main reasons: First, all states require a licence to practice land surveying. Second, your friend or survey technician will not be allowed to defend your claim in court, as they would be practising land surveying without a licence.

10. There Is a Special Point of Beginning from Which All Land Measurement Is Taken From

This depends largely on some descriptions of the land. Some take measurement from source whilst others do not. For example, for platted or subdivided lots, there is no such special point; all lots are created simultaneously.

11. All Land Surveys Are Easy and Quick

This is determined by the land in question; its shape, size, geographical positions, etc. But your mindset and schedule may also play a part in determining when to complete the work.

12. All Land Surveys Now Use GPS and GIS with a Common Coordinate System

Though many land surveyors use *global positioning system* (GPS) and *geographic information systems* (GIS), many are also not required to. Normally, the instrument and machine to use in surveying depends on the requirements of the land survey and compliance with applicable local ordinances or state laws.

13. I Don't Need a Land Survey Because I Found My "Stake"

The land surveyor is basically employed and paid by you to confirm that what you may have found is really your property corner. In the course of surveying, the land surveyor may end up identifying multiple corners or just plain bogus corners all within a foot and a half radius.

14. I Don't Need a Land Survey to Construct a Fence or Build on My Land

There is law with regard to land; its use, acquisition, easement, and others in every state. To protect your investment, you must ensure it complies with the laws of the country, and this can only be done by a licenced land surveyor.

15. I Can Construct a New Fence or Wall Right on the Property Line

The question is, can you maintain it without trespassing? Do the footings encroach? Can you build that accurately? To avoid any further land disputes and clarify things, verify from local building and zoning regulations, which often have requirements to help and protect everyone, including you.

16. I Own the Property to the Sidewalk or to the Back of the Curb of the Street

Normally, a lot of land has right of way for streets and utilities.

17. If a Street Next to Me Is Not Used Anymore, Can I Get Half of That Land?

This is not advisable because it is possible that the road may be vacated. Check from land authorities. This situation may be referred to as reversionary rights, which do not always revert to the adjoiner.

18. A Land Surveyor Will Surely Side with My Understanding of the Property Line in Question, Not My Neighbor's, Because I Hired Him

The work of the land surveyor is to determine the property lines correctly, not necessarily your way.

19. I Can Disagree with a Land Surveyor Who Determines My Property Lines and Hire Another Land Surveyor Who Will Satisfy My Need.

You don't pay a land surveyor simply to persuade him/her to agree with your wish regarding the property line.

20. I Was Told Where My Lines Were When I Purchased My Land. What Is the Big Deal?

A land surveyor is the only person qualified to determine your property corners, so it is of no big deal for a land surveyor to tell you where the lines were.

21. Land Surveyors Work Very Efficiently in All Sorts of Weather and Conditions. They Must Be Virtually Indestructible and Almost Superhuman

Don't we wish land surveyors do work outside in most weather? Most land surveyors have learned not to complain about the weather; that is nature. It must be emphasised working in adverse conditions hamper the efficiency of the land survey.

22. Somebody Removed My Property Corner. Isn't There a Law against That?

Normally, this is covered in states' statutory laws. Refer to that.

CHAPTER SEVEN

PROPERTY RIGHTS OF SPOUSES

Who gets what in divorce battles can be one of the most difficult decisions a judge will have to make. These proceedings tend to be acrimonious, as each spouse is bent on benefitting as much as possible from the property distribution to be made by the court. But the bases for such distributions have varied over the years.

Before Ghana achieved independence status and the period around the independence era, the law was every property acquired during marriage belonged to the husband. This was the position, whether the property was acquired solely by the husband or jointly by the husband and the wife, and the properties acquired by the husband with assistance of the wife or children belonged to the husband exclusively (Brobbey 2015). This assertion was given effect in the case of *Quartey v Martey* [1959] GLR 377. It was further held by the court that the proceeds of this joint effort of a man and his wife and/or children, and any property which the man acquires with such proceeds, are, by customary law, the individual property of the man. It is not the joint property of the man and the wife and/or the children. By customary law, it is the duty of a man's wife and children to assist him in carrying out of the duties of his station in life. On the one hand, the only duty of the husband was to cater for the wife and children whilst he enjoys the right and interest in land and other immovable properties alone.

This aspect of the customary law has met widespread criticism. In hindsight, it is clear this practise was unfair and insensitive towards women, taking into cognizance the various roles our women played for their husbands to acquiring these properties. It is even said equity and good conscience ought not to support such cruel and unjust treatment. The law determines everything in a society. It is in this regard that there has been a sharp contrast to our customary law in recent times. This positive development has come in handy as it helps correct the ills in our legal system.

Before the coming into force of the *1992 Constitution*, women suffered multiple discrimination and deprivation when it came to sharing of spousal property. Article 22 was, therefore, deliberately enacted to correct the sins of the past and bring into the realm of equity access to provision from the estate of a spouse, whether the spouse died having made a will. It was also required, per Article 22 (2), that parliament should, as soon as practicable, after the coming into force of the constitution, enact legislation regulating the property rights of spouses. Article 22 (3) boldly outlines the principle that (A) joint acquisition of spousal property shall have equal access and (B) assets acquired jointly during marriage shall be distributed equitably between the spouses upon the dissolution of the marriage.

The rationale behind the constitutional provisions on right of spouses to property is to right the imbalances women have historically suffered in the distribution of assets jointly acquired during marriage. An equal distribution will often be a solution to this imbalance.

The new *Lands Act 2020 (Act 1036)* has, therefore, given effect to the constitutional provision. Section 38 (3) and (4) provide that "In a conveyance for valuable consideration of an interest in land that is jointly acquired during marriage, the spouses shall be deemed to be parties to the conveyance, unless a contrary intention is expressed in the conveyance. Where contrary to subsection (3) a conveyance is made to only one spouse that spouse shall be presumed to be holding the land in trust for the spouses unless a contrary intention is expressed in the conveyance".

This new provision has moved away from the previous legal position that properties acquired by a man together with his wife is his personal property. The new law is to the effect that unless it is expressly stated that the property belongs to the husband or wife alone, it is presumed any conveyance for valuable consideration of an interest in land is jointly acquired during marriage. Therefore, during the subsistence of a marriage, any property acquired belongs to both spouses. It will, therefore, be in order for both spouses to have a fair and equitable share during dissolution of the marriage.

Section 47 of the act also protects the rights of property of spouses. It stipulates that, except as provided for in subsections 3 and 4 of section 38, in the absence of a written agreement to the contrary by the spouses in a marriage, a spouse shall not, in respect of land right or interest in land acquired for valuable consideration during marriage,

(a) Sell, exchange, transfer, mortgage or lease the land, right or interest in land;

(b) Enter into a contract for sale, exchange, transfer, mortgage or lease of the land, right or interest in the land;

(c) Give away the land or interest in the land inter vivos; or

(d) Enter into other transaction in relation to the land, right or interest in the land without the written consent of the other spouse, which consent shall not be unreasonably withheld.

The general understanding to this new provision is that a spouse cannot sell, transfer, mortgage or lease land, or give away in the form of a gift whilst both are alive. This is to the effect that you will need the consent of your spouse before any transaction of a sort can be carried out on an interest in land. Without that, any sale, exchange, transfer or gift of land, right, or interest in land jointly acquired is void. It can clearly be seen this is a sharp contrast to the old legal position where a husband enjoyed personally the right and interest in land and other immovable properties. To this end, it can rightly be said the law is going in the right direction as it catches up with modern and contemporary practices.

The supreme court has also played a major role in making sure these laws are given effect through their decisions. The supreme court as a court of law and equity has applied the "equality is equity" principle to favour women in benefitting from properties acquired in a marriage. In *Gladys Mensah v Stephen Mensah* [2012] 1 SCGLR 391, Dotse JSC held that the woman's contribution, even as a housewife in maintaining the house and creating a congenial atmosphere for the husband to create the empire he built, is enough for her to earn an equal share in marital property. The court defined marital property as any property acquired during marriage.

However, a gift received by a spouse during a marriage does not become a marital property. This is to address an important caution to the effect that the jurisprudence of equality is not an open sea to fish from; the circumstances and specific facts will determine the applicability.

The supreme court's previous decision in *Mensah v Mensah* is not to be taken as a blanket ruling that affords spouses unwarranted access to property when it is clear on the evidence that they are not so entitled. The principle is to avoid unwarranted access to property that a spouse is not entitled to. The recognition in the new Lands Act 2020 (Act 1036) gives further weight to spousal property right. After *Mensah v Mensah* (supra), the issue before us is how to determine the context within which to apply the equitable maxim of equality is equity. There is no doubt the courts have come a long way in the development of the law on marital property. For much of the time, the courts have been ahead of the legislature. They have established principles that make it easier for parties to predict what the outcome of a case before a judge would be.

CHAPTER EIGHT

EXTRACT FROM THE GHANA LAND ACT 2020 (ACT 1036)

On 23 December 2020, the Land Act 2020 (Act 1036) became operational in Ghana. The act updates and unifies earlier land-related laws into a single piece of legislation, and it represents the culmination of land-related reforms that started with the introduction of the 1999 National Land Policy (NLP). The act's stated goal is to ensure effective and efficient land tenure, sustainable land administration, and management. Amongst other things, it does this by establishing a broad-based framework for registering land rights and interests, a framework for customary land rights, and increasing transparency and accountability in land governance institutions.

Transaction-Based Registration and Recording of Land Rights

The act establishes three systems for the recording and registration of rights and interests in land, namely the recording of customary rights and interests of the Customary Land Secretariats (CLS), the registration of instruments pertaining to land, and the registration of title, interests, and rights to land. According to the act, registrable rights include mortgages, easements, restrictive covenants, profit a prendre, powers of attorney, contractual licences, and user rights under a certificate of allocation. Additionally, registrable interests include allodial title, common law freehold, customary law freehold, usufructuary interest, leasehold interest, and customary tenancy as well as an interest in a condominium, an apartment, or flat2. Alternative dispute resolution has been implemented as the dispute resolution mechanism in situations involving land or interests in land registration districts to expedite the registration process and relieve the burden on the land courts. This is intended to take the place of the Land Title Registration Act of 1986's ineffective title adjudication committees (PNDCL 152)

- **Customary Land Rights Framework**

The Act makes significant improvements in setting out the legal framework for customary land rights. For instance, those in charge of managing the lands belonging to the stool, skin, family, or clan are now referred to as fiduciaries and have a responsibility to carry out their duties in the stool, skin, family, or clan's best interests. The law requires them to make judgements affecting land in a transparent, open, just, and impartial manner since they are fiduciaries. Any such fiduciary who violates his/her fiduciary obligations will be punished with a fine and/or imprisonment to promote compliance.

Additionally, the act gives a new legal basis for the Customary Land Secretariats (CLS) and assigns to them the responsibility of taking an inventory of customary rights, transactions, and interests within their jurisdiction. Up 'til then, legislation on customary land administration was confined to only stool and skin lands. Clan and family holdings have now been incorporated into the customary land provisions to create a unitary system of customary land administration.

Electronic Conveyancing

In an effort to expedite the conveyancing procedure, the act introduced electronic conveyancing. To enable the electronic transfer, creation, and registration of land interests, the Lands Commission is required to build a land information system with the necessary information technology infrastructure. The following, amongst others, are necessary conditions for an authorised electronic conveyance:

(i) The electronic conveyance is to be made by a qualified legal practitioner who has been granted access to the information system by the Lands Commission;
(ii) The electronic conveyance must record the time and date on which the conveyance takes effect; and
(iii) The electronic signature of each person who authenticates the conveyance and each electronic signature on the conveyance must be certified in accordance with the Electronic Transactions Act 2008 (Act 772).

Defending Spousal Rights

The act significantly strengthens the protection of spousal land rights in the context of land acquired during marriage in accordance with Article 22 of Ghana's 1992 Constitution. For instance, unless a different intention is expressed, spouses' names must be included when registering land acquired for valuable consideration during marriage, and any land acquired during marriage by one spouse is presumed to be owned jointly by both spouses, even if only one spouse's name is registered.

For transactions involving land acquired for a valuable consideration whilst a couple is married, the act also mandates spousal permission. In accordance with Section 47 of the act, a spouse may not, in relation to land, rights, or interests in land obtained for valuable consideration during marriage, the land, a right, or interest therein, may be sold, exchanged, transferred, mortgaged, or leased,

- enter into a contract for the sale, exchange, transfer, mortgage or lease of the land, right, or interest in the land;
- give away the land, right, or interest in the land inter vivos; or
- enter into any other transaction in relation to the land, right, or interest in the land without the written consent of the other spouse, which consent shall not be unreasonably withheld. This clause is consistent with Ghana's Sustainable Development Goal (SDG) No. 5, which calls for reforms to grant women equitable access to economic resources, including land and other types of property, financial services, inheritance, and natural resources in conformity with national laws.

- **Enhancing Transparency, Accountability, and Accessibility in Land Governance Institutions**

The act stipulates particular sanctions for violations by land sector authorities and other people in an effort to promote sustainable land administration and management. Falsification of land records, fraudulent issuance, entry, erasure, or alteration of documents issued by the Lands Commission, fraudulent mutilation or obliteration of any land register or other document kept in the Lands Commission, and fraudulent deletion or alteration of the Lands Commission's electronic records by a public officer or any other person are all prohibited under the act.

In summary, the new act offers a crucial opportunity to address historical and present challenges and issues in the land sector for national development in light of Ghana's economic progress and population growth. New innovations, like electronic conveyancing, are Ghana's response to the fast-paced global environment and are anticipated to increase the effectiveness of recording and registering land transactions.

CHAPTER NINE

BIBLICAL QUOTES ABOUT LAND AND BOUNDARIES

Land is believed by Christians to be a special gift from God and most powerful asset of creation. The next to heaven is land per Genesis 1:1 of the Holy Bible. Land contains minerals, water bodies, living and non-living things, etc. Bible is, therefore, not quite about land and, therefore, has the following guidelines about land use:

1. **Deuteronomy 19:14 (NKJV)**

You shall not remove your neighbor's landmark, which the men of old have set, in your inheritance which you will inherit in the land that the LORD your God is giving you to possess.

2. **Deuteronomy 27:17 (NKJV)**

Cursed is the one who moves his neighbor's landmark. And all the people shall say, "Amen!"

3. **Proverbs 22:28 (NKJV)**

Do not remove the ancient landmark which your fathers have set.

4. **Numbers 34:6 (NKJV)**

As for the western border, you shall have the Great Sea for a border; this shall be your western border.

5. **Ezekiel 42:16–19 (NKJV)**

He measured the east side with the measuring rod, five hundred rods by the measuring rod all around. He measured the north side, five hundred rods by the measuring rod all around. He measured the south side, five hundred rods by the measuring rod. He came around to the west side and measured five hundred rods by the measuring rod.

6. **Revelation 21:16–17 (NKJV)**

The city is laid out as a square; its length is as great as its breadth. And he measured the city with the reed: twelve thousand furlongs. Its length, breadth, and height are equal. Then he measured its wall: one hundred and forty-four cubits, according to the measure of a man, that is, of an angel.

7. Zechariah 2:1–2 (NKJV)

Then I raised my eyes and looked, and behold, a man with a measuring line in his hand. So I said, "Where are you going?" And he said to me, "To measure Jerusalem, to see what is its width and what is its length". Thereof, and what is the length thereof.

8. Job 24:2 (NKJV)

Some remove landmarks; they seize flocks violently and feed on them.

9. Leviticus 25:23–28 (NKJV)

"The land, moreover, shall not be sold permanently, for the land is Mine; for you are but aliens and sojourners with Me." Thus for every piece of your property, you are to provide for the redemption of the land. 'If a fellow countryman of yours becomes so poor he has to sell part of his property, then his nearest kinsman is to come and buy back what his relative has sold.

10. Numbers 33:53–54 (NKJV)

You shall take possession of the land and live in it, for I have given the land to you to possess it. 'You shall inherit the land by lot according to your families; to the larger you shall give more inheritance, and to the smaller you shall give less inheritance. Wherever the lot falls to anyone that shall be his. You shall inherit according to the tribes of your fathers.

11. Genesis 47:20 (NKJV)

So Joseph bought all the land of Egypt for Pharaoh, for every Egyptian sold his field, because the famine was severe

12. Leviticus 20:24 (NKJV)

"Hence I have said to you, 'You are to possess their land, and I Myself will give it to you to possess it, a land flowing with upon them. Thus the land became Pharaoh's.

milk and honey" I am the LORD your God, who has separated you from the peoples.

13. Numbers 34:12 (NKJV)

The border shall go down along the Jordan, and it shall end at the Salt Sea. This shall be your land with its surrounding boundaries.

14. Proverbs 23:10 (NKJV)

Do not move the ancient boundary Or go into the fields of the fatherless.

15. Hosea 5:10 (NKJV)

The princes of Judah have become like those who move a boundary; On them I will pour out My wrath like water.

16. Numbers 34:6 (NKJV)

As for the western border, you shall have the Great Sea for a border; this shall be your western border.

17. Genesis 10:5 (NKJV)

By these were the isles of the Gentiles divided in their lands; everyone after his tongue, after their families, in their nations.

18. Numbers 35:33–34 (NIV)

^{33} "'Do not pollute the land where you are. Bloodshed pollutes the land, and atonement cannot be made for the land on which blood has been shed, except by the blood of the one who shed it. ^{34} Do not defile the land where you live and where I dwell, for I, the Lord, dwell among the Israelites.'"

19. Leviticus 20:24 (NIV)

²⁴ But I said to you, "You will possess their land; I will give it to you as an inheritance, a land flowing with milk and honey." I am the Lord your God, who has set you apart from the nations.

20. Genesis 50:24

And Joseph said unto his brethren, I die: and God will surely visit you, and bring you out of this land unto the land which he sware to Abraham, to Isaac, and to Jacob.

CHAPTER TEN

ISLAMIC RELIGION LANDOWNERSHIP

In Islam, it is generally acknowledged that Allah (SWT) is the Creator-Owner and Lord Sovereign of "all that is in the heavens and on the earth". Furthermore, he has delegated to man the power and authority to utilise and exploit the resources he has kindly bestowed upon them (Salasai 1998).

The rights of the owner over a property, such as land, in Islam are stipulated in the Shari'ah law. The Shari'ah also affords its protection by laying down rules and regulations so owners and other individuals would be guided and will not abuse the power and authority thereby accorded to them (Salasai 1998).

According to Igbal and Gill (2000), land in the Islamic countries are generally of two categories: owned and unowned.

1. Owned land or private land: In this type of landownership, the owners of land are converted to Islam at the time of conquest; the property will remain with such owners and "Ushr" will be levied on them, in case of agricultural lands. Also, owners may not convert to Islam but, by way of peace and compromise, surrender to the obedience of Muslim rule. Terms and conditions or facts of the compromise are honoured forever.
2. Unowned land or unclaimed land: This type of land is not owned by any person but is used for the common benefit of all the residents of a locality or from which certain things of common use, like salt, kerosene oil, petrol, etc., is being extracted. Such property shall forever remain open for public use under the supervision of the Muslim government or authority.

Kinds and type of landownership: There are about six types of landownership namely: Fay' lands, Khassa or exclusive lands, Hima land (collective reserves for grazing of cattle), AK-IQTĀ (grant or benefice or a piece of land), Ihyā Al-Mawāt (bringing uncultivated and dead land to life), and Bay lands (transaction).

The Islamic teachings have authorised five various forms of tenancy namely: free tenure, partnership tenure, lease of bare land, Muzāara'a tenancy, and labour tenancy.

In Islam, everything, including the being of man, is owned by God. Land and its plentiful provisions belong to him but have been given to man to keep in trust, to be used wisely for his own benefit and that of the larger community.

For example, the Quran says, "To Him belongs what is in the heavens and what is on the earth and what is between them and what is under the soil" (20:6), whilst it also observes that "It is He who made the earth tame for you — so walk among its slopes and eat of His provision — and to Him is the resurrection" (67:15).

To promote entrepreneurship and human creativity, Islam has encouraged private holdings of such resources that may be in excess and are not held at the cost of people's welfare.

The Quran does not lay out specific instructions on how land may be distributed, but it does spell out the principles clearly for a fair and just system to be developed in an Islamic society.

In Islam, it is generally acknowledged that Allah (SWT) is the Creator-Owner and Lord Sovereign of "all that is in the heavens and on the earth". Land, like everything, belongs to him. Like water, air, and sunshine, land is meant for the common use and benefit of the community.2 Furthermore, he has delegated to man the power and authority to utilise and exploit the resources he has kindly bestowed upon them.

The basic principle envisaged in Islam relating to landownership is the concept that land vests solely in Allah (SWT). That is, land, as a free and universal gift from Allah, must be utilised to the fullest. It was also given to men for their common use as well as for the general welfare of the society. The following *ayat* from the Holy Quran clearly reflect the above contention. Allah (SWT) has said that

"All that is in the heavens and on the earth belong to Allah (SWT)" (S-An-Nisa (4):126 & 134).

"To him belongs whatever is in the heavens and on earth" (Surah An-Nahl (16): 52).

"His is the Kingdom of the heavens and the earth and all that lies between them" (Surah al-Zukhruf (43): 85; Surah Al-Maidah (5): 120).8

"It is He who has made the earth manageable for you so traverse you through its tracts and enjoy of the sustenance which he fumishes, but unto Him is the resurrection" (Surah al-Mulk (67): 15).

CHAPTER ELEVEN

SOCIAL QUOTES ABOUT LAND AND BOUNDARIES

1. The land is the only thing in the world worth working for, worth fighting for, worth dying for because it's the only thing that lasts, Gerald O'Hara, *Gone with the Wind*. **(Margaret Mitchell)**
2. Ancestral power is lost and posterity is cut off when a native land is sold. **(E A Gyamera)**
3. Owning a piece of land is for posterity and economic empowerment; at least own one. **(E A Gyamera)**
4. Land sold is power sold; lease it instead. **(E A Gyamera)**
5. Do not rush to acquire land without an expert's advice. You might regret. **(E A Gyamera)**
6. What greater grief than the loss of one's native land. **(Euripides)**
7. Buy land, they're not making it anymore. **(Mark Twain)**
8. Oceans separate lands, not souls. **(Munia Khan)**
9. Until we understand what the land is, we are at odds with everything we touch. And to come to that understanding, it is necessary, even now, to leave the regions of our conquest—the cleared fields, the towns

and cities, the highways—and reenter the woods. For only there can a man encounter the silence and the darkness of his own absence. Only in this silence and darkness can he recover the sense of the world's longevity, of its ability to thrive without him, of his inferiority to it and his dependence on it. **(Wendell Berry, The Art of the Commonplace: The Agrarian Essay)**

10. The land belongs to the future, Carl; that's the way it seems to me. How many of the names on the county clerk's plat will be there in 50 years? I might as well try to will the sunset over there to my brother's children. We come and go, but the land is always here. And the people who love it and understand it are the people who own it—for a little while. **(Willa Cather, *O Pioneers!*)**
11. Never, never, and never again shall it be that this beautiful land will again experience the oppression of one by another. **(Nelson Mandela)**
12. When the missionaries came to Africa, they had the Bible, and we had the land. They said, "Let us pray". We closed our eyes. When we opened them, we had the Bible, and they had the land. **(Desmond Tutu)**
13. We abuse land because we regard it as a commodity belonging to us. When we see land as a community to which we belong, we may begin to use it with love and respect. **(Aldo Leopold)**
14. We know our lands have now become more valuable. The white people think we do not know their value, but we know that the land is everlasting, and the few goods we receive for it are soon worn out and gone. **(Canasatego)**

15. Land is the secure ground of home; the sea is like life, the outside, the unknown. **(Stephen Gardiner)**
16. Although the life of a person is in a land full of thorns and weeds, there is always a space in which the good seed can grow. You have to trust God. **(Pope Francis)**
17. Conservation is a state of harmony between men and land. **(Aldo Leopold)**
18. As a former mayor, I know that local governments must have control over land use decision. **(Elton Gallegly)**
19. To have good farming or good land use of any kind, you have got to have limits. Capitalism doesn't acknowledge limits. **(Wendell Berry)**
20. As with nearly all proposed development standards, the goal is to encourage efficient land use, flexibility, and a wide variety of housing types whilst reducing the potential for negative impacts. **(Bill Vaughan)**
21. You have got to connect your land use decisions with transportation decisions. **(Tim Kaine)**
22. Property is intended to serve life, and no matter how much we surround it with rights and respects, it has no personal being. It is part of the earth man walks on. It is no man. **(Martin Luther King Jr.)**
23. Each blade of grass has its spot on earth whence it draws its life, its strength; and so is man rooted to the land from which he draws his faith together with his life. **(Joseph Conrad)**
24. No pessimist ever discovered the secret of the stars, or sailed to an uncharted land, or opened a new doorway for the human spirit. **(Helen Keller)**
25. Whenever there is a conflict between human rights and property rights, human rights must prevail. **(Abraham Lincoln)**

26. If a man own land, the land owns him. **(Ralph Waldo Emerson)**
27. It is through this mysterious power that we too have our being, and we therefore yield to our neighbors, even to our animal neighbors, the same right as ourselves to inhabit this vast land. **(Sitting Bull)**
28. A land ethic, then, reflects the existence of an ecological conscience, and this in turn reflects a conviction of individual responsibility for the health of the land. Health is the capacity of the land for self-renewal. Conservation is our effort to understand and preserve this capacity. **(Wendell Berry)**
29. Where water is boss, the land must obey. **(African Proverb)**
30. This is my homeland; no one can kick me out. **(Yasser Arafat)**
31. All are kings of this land. **(Subramanya Bharathi)**
32. No man acquires property without acquiring with it a little arithmetic also. **(Ralph Waldo Emerson)**
33. To every people the land is given on condition. Perceived or not, there is a covenant, beyond the constitution, beyond sovereign guarantee, beyond the nation's sweetest dreams of itself. **(Leonard Cohen)**
34. So long as the great majority of men are not deprived of either property or honour, they are satisfied. **(Niccolo Machiavelli)**
35. This land is your land and this land is my land, sure, but the world is run by those that never listen to music anyway. **(Bob Dylan)**
36. The major fortunes in America have been made in land. **(John D. Rockefeller)**

37. It is a comfortable feeling to know that you stand on your own ground. Land is about the only thing that can't fly away. **(Anthony Trollope)**
38. The nation that destroys its soil destroys itself. **(Franklin Delano Roosevelt)**
39. The small landholders are the most precious part of a state. **(Thomas Jefferson)**
40. Drink is the curse of the land. It makes you fight with your neighbor. It makes you shoot at your landlord and it makes you miss him. **(Irish Proverb)**
41. Land really is the best art. **(Andy Warhol)**
42. Apply yourself both now and in the next life. Without effort, you cannot be prosperous. Though the land can be good, you cannot have an abundant crop without cultivation. **(Plato)**
43. Land: A part of the earth's surface, considered as property. The theory that land is property subject to private ownership and control is the foundation of modern society, and is eminently worthy of the superstructure. **(Ambrose Bierce)**
44. The chief who bullies the landowners starts by breaking his sugarcane. **(Ugandan Proverb)**
    a. **Food for Thought**

The following advice must be taken seriously:

1) It is advisable for everyone to own at least one plot of land.
2) Every acquired land must be registered at Lands Commission.
3) If you have acquired a land and it is not registered and you are not making any arrangement to register, then you must assume you have no land.

4) It is advisable to acquire land through a solicitor or a registered land consultant.
5) You can acquire government land through the Lands Commission only.
6) You can go to the Lands Commission and register your land without any land agent.
7) Beware of *hot cake* lands.
8) Before you collect your documents, ask officials of the Lands Commission whether final registration has been done.
9) Make sure your document is registered at the deed registry before you collect it.
10) An unregistered document is no security of title. It is not accepted in court.
11) Banks do not accept unregistered documents. Have your documents registered!
12) Anyone who has acquired land and has not presented it at the Lands Commission for processing and registration is taking a dangerous risk.
13) Land transactions that are not registered with the Lands Commission are just mere papers and are of no legal effect.
14) By registering your documents at Lands Commission, proper title is conferred on you.

CHAPTER TWELVE

SOME BASIC TERMINOLOGIES IN SURVEYING

1. **Acre** - a measure of land, 160 square rods (4,480 square yards; 43,560 square feet) in whatever shape, 208.7103' square.
2. **Angle** - the difference in direction between two convergent lines. It may be classed as horizontal, vertical, oblique, spherical, or spheroidal, according to whether it is measured in a horizontal, vertical, or inclined plane or in a curved surface.
3. **Barleycorn** - an old measure of length, equal to the average length of a grain of barley; the third part of an inch.
4. **Base lines** - a surveyed line established with more than usual care, to which surveys are referred for coordination and correction.
5. **Bearing** - the direction of one point or object, with respect to another, where the acute angle is with respect to a reference meridian. The reference direction can be north or south and the meridian may be assumed, grid, magnetic, astronomic, or geodetic. Typical bearings are N 60°, 10'E, S 31°, 17' W, N 17° 22'W.
6. **Benchmark (BM)** - a relatively permanent material object, natural or artificial, bearing a marked point whose elevation above or below an adopted datum is known. Usually designated as a BM, such a mark is sometimes qualified as a *permanent benchmark* (PBM) to distinguish it from a *temporary benchmark* (TBM),

which is a mark less permanent in character intended to serve for only a comparatively short time.

7. **Boundary monument** - a material object placed on or near a boundary line to preserve and identify the location of the boundary line on the ground. Where it is impracticable to establish a monument on or very close to a boundary line on the ground, it is preserved by reference marks. The term monument is sometimes used to include the mark on the boundary line and the reference mark.

8. **Cardinal direction** - the directions on the surface of the earth: north, south, east, and west. The term cardinal, without qualification, is sometimes used to indicate any or all the above directions, the context giving the exact meaning to its use.

9. **Chain** – a unit of length used in the subdivision of public lands of the United States. The Gunter's Chain is 66 feet long and is divided into 100 links, each 7.92 inches long. In its earliest construction, the chain was made from iron, later heavy steel wire, in short pieces bent at the end to form rings; three extra rings were placed in between the pieces in each assembly to make up a whole link or 7.92 inches. There are many wearing surfaces and other ready causes for errors in length. The link chain was not superseded by the steel ribbon tape, in general practice, until after 1900. The chain is a convenient length for land measurement because 10 square chains is equal to an acre*. Compare *link*.

10. **Common law** - The body of judicial decisions developed in England and based upon immemorial usage. It is an unwritten law as opposed to statute or written law. The English common law forms the foundation for the system of law in the United States.

11. **Cubit** - a measure of length, in its origin the length of the forearm from the elbow to the extremity of the middle finger; in English measure, 18 inches (45.72 cm). The Ancient Egyptian cubit was 20.7 inches (52.5 cm), and the Ancient Roman cubit was 17.5 inches (44.36 cm). The usual cubit of the Ancient Greeks is stated to have been 18.22 inches (46.29 cm), and the Hebrews, 17.58 inches (44.65 cm). The cubit is also known as *hath* in India; *covid* in the East; *codo* in Spain; *hasta* in the Ancient Hindu system, etc.
12. **Datum** - any numerical or geometrical quantity or set of such quantities that may serve as a reference or base for other quantities. For a group of statistical references, the plural form is data as geographic data for list of latitudes and longitudes. Where the concept is geometrical and particular, rather than statistical and inclusive, the plural form is datums.
13. **Datum, mean sea level** - a determination of mean sea level that has been adopted as a standard datum for heights or elevations. The sea level datum of 1929, the current standard datum for geodetic leveling in the United States, is based on tidal observations over a number of years at various tide stations along the coasts.
14. **Evidence** - that which is legally submitted to a competent tribunal as a means of ascertaining the truth of any alleged matter of fact under investigation before it; means of making proof; medium of proof.
15. **Eyott** – a small island arising in a river
16. **Fathom** - (1) a unit of distance equivalent to 6 feet, used primarily in marine measurements; (2) to find the depth of something; to sound.

17. **Flood plain** - (1) valley land along the course of a stream subject to inundation during periods of high water that exceed normal bank-full elevation; (2) land that is parallel to the stream with approximately level ground elevation, gentle longitudinal slope corresponding to the gradient of the stream, and very flat backslope; (3) natural terrain frequency consisting of low-lying timbered land, interspersed with swamp, marsh, small lakes, ponds, and bayous.
18. **Four-pole chain** – a pole is 16.5 feet; a four-pole Chain is, therefore, 66 feet; also termed as Gunter's Chain.
19. **Furlong** - a measure of length equal to a quarter of a mile or 220 yards.
20. **Grantee** - a person to whom property is transferred by *deed* or to whom property rights are granted by a trust instrument or other document.
21. **Great Pond** in Maine and Massachusetts, natural ponds (lakes) having an area of more than 10 acres.
22. **Land surveying** - the art or science of (1) reestablishing cadastral surveys and land boundaries based on documents of record and historical evidence; (2) planning, designing, and establishing property boundaries; and (3) certifying surveys as required by statute or local ordinance, such as subdivision plats, registered land surveys, judicial surveys, and space delineation. Land surveying can include associated services, such as mapping and related data accumulation; construction layout surveys; precision measurements of length, angle, elevation, area, and volume; horizontal and vertical control systems, and the analysis and utilisation of survey data.

23. **Link** - a unit of linear measure, 100th of a chain and equivalent to 7.92 inches. Compare *chain*.
24. **Metes and bounds** - a method of describing land by measure of length (metes) of the boundary lines (bounds). Most common method is to recite direction and length of each line as one would walk around the perimeter. In general, the "metes" and "bounds" can be recited by reference to record natural or artificial monuments at the corners and record natural or cultural boundary lines.
25. **Palm** - a unit of measure where a palm is equal to 3 inches to 4 inches (United States); 3.94 inches (Netherlands).
26. **Peonia** - in Spanish law, a portion of land formally given to a simple soldier on the conquest of a country. It is now a quantity of land of different provinces. In the Spanish possessions in America, it is measured 50 feet front and 100 feet deep.
27. **Perch** - a measure of length, varying locally in different countries but by statute in Great Britain and the United States, equal to 16.5 feet. It was used extensively in the early public land surveys and is equivalent in length to a rod or pole.
28. **Pied** - one-sixth of a toise.
29. **Rod** - (1) a measure of length containing 5.5 yards or 16.5 feet; (2) the corresponding square measure, called also perch or pole; (3) any slender bar as of wood or metal, specifically a bar or staff for measuring.
30. **Rood** - (1) a square measure of equal, in England and Scotland, usually to one-fourth of an acre, or 40 square rods; in the Union of South Africa, to 17.07 square yards

or 14.28 square meters; (2) a linear measure varying locally, from 5.5 to 8 yards.
31. **Span** - 1 span = 6 inches
32. **Survey, Cadastral** - a survey relating to land boundaries and subdivision made to create units suitable for transfer or to define the limitations of title. Derived from "cadastre", which means register of the real property of a political subdivision with details of area, ownership, and value. The term cadastral survey is now used to designate the surveys of the public lands of the United States, including retracement surveys for the identification and resurveys for the restoration of property lines; the term can also be applied properly to corresponding surveys outside public lands, although such surveys are usually termed land surveys through preference.
33. **Toise** - a unit of length used in early geodetic surveys and equal to about 6.4 English feet.
34. **Verst** - a Russian measure of distance equal to 0.6629 mile or 1.067 kilometres.
35. **Westa** - half a hide of land or 60 acres.

CHAPTER 13

GOVERNMENT POLICIES AND LAND ADMINISTRATION REFORM

13.1 National Land Policy Overview

Ghana's land policy framework represents an intricate tapestry woven from the threads of its historical legacies, socio-political dynamics, and the urgent contemporary necessity to manage scarce land resources efficiently and equitably. The evolution of this framework reflects the country's ongoing quest to balance customary land tenure systems, which are deeply entrenched in the cultural fabric of Ghanaian society, with statutory laws designed to foster clarity, security, and economic development. At its core, the National Land Policy is rooted in the understanding that land is not merely a physical asset but a powerful symbol of identity, authority, and opportunity, and as such, its governance demands a multi-layered, nuanced, and inclusive approach.

The earliest organized attempts at establishing a coherent land policy in Ghana trace back to post-independence efforts focused on reconciling the indigenous systems of landholding with the modernizing imperatives of a nascent nation. These initial frameworks sought to integrate customary tenure practices, which had historically governed the majority of rural lands, with statutory provisions intended to facilitate registration, documentation, and formalized ownership. The government recognized that without formal registration and clear legal recognition, disputes would persist, undermining social harmony and stalling economic potential. This recognition paved the way for successive policy reforms aimed at improving land administration structures, streamlining registration processes, and reducing fragmented jurisdiction between various land institutions.

One of the pivotal milestones in Ghana's land policy development came with the enactment of the 1992 Constitution, which underscored the importance of land as a national asset, while explicitly acknowledging the rightful place of customary authorities in land management. This constitutional framework set the tone for subsequent legislative and policy initiatives by affirming that while the state holds sovereign custodianship over all land, ownership and control rest primarily with the stools, skins, and families in accordance with customary law. The Constitution thereby entrenched a dual system of land tenure – customary and statutory – that demands coordination and harmonization rather than outright replacement of traditional structures.

The 1999 National Land Policy marked a transformative moment in Ghana's land governance by articulating a comprehensive vision for the sustainable utilization and equitable distribution of land resources. This policy was designed to address the multifarious challenges that had beset the sector, including opaque ownership records, rampant encroachment, disputes arising from overlapping claims, and inefficient land market transactions. Central to this policy's ethos was the principle of decentralization: empowering local land agencies and traditional leadership to operate transparently within the broader legal framework. By advocating for collaborative governance between customary institutions and state agencies, the policy sought to create a balance between respecting traditional rights and ensuring conformity to statutory regulations.

A core component of the National Land Policy lies in its strengthening of the land registration system, recognizing that the absence of secure tenure documentation lies at the heart of many conflicts. The policy calls for the transformation of the existing registration system, which had been criticized for its bureaucratic delays and corruption vulnerabilities, into a computerized, accessible registry managed by the Land Commission. The introduction of the Land Title Registration Law and subsequent reforms pursued the format of the Torrens system, a land title registration model that guarantees indefeasible titles, thereby providing owners with legal certainty. This shift was anticipated to reduce the incidences of competing claims and fraudulent transactions, both of which have historically exacerbated conflicts and discouraged investment.

Alongside formalizing ownership documentation, the National Land Policy places significant emphasis on transparency and accountability mechanisms within land administration. Recognizing that mismanagement and opaque procedures have fueled mistrust between stakeholders, the policy advocates for the establishment of comprehensive guidelines to ensure that land allocations and sales are conducted openly, following clear criteria that safeguard public interest and traditional rights. Community participation is given paramount importance, with mechanisms envisioned to involve local stakeholders, including chiefs, elders, women, and youth groups, in decision-making processes related to land allocation and dispute resolution. This participatory approach is critical for aligning policy ambitions with ground realities and fostering social cohesion.

Furthermore, the policy draws attention to the need for effective conflict prevention and resolution mechanisms. Rather than solely reacting to disputes when they arise, the framework underscores proactive approaches aimed at early identification and mediation of potential conflicts. This includes recommendations for strengthening the capacity of customary authorities and local government entities to manage land disputes through culturally sensitive, expedient, and cost-effective methods. The policy envisions integrating alternative dispute resolution processes, such as mediation and negotiation, alongside formal judicial proceedings to alleviate the burden on courts and expedite resolutions.

One of the policy's remarkable features is its focus on gender inclusivity and social equity within land governance. Historically, women in many Ghanaian communities have faced systemic barriers to land access and ownership due to patrilineal inheritance customs and discriminatory practices. The National Land Policy explicitly calls for reforms to dismantle such disparities, promoting legal recognition of women's rights to inherit, purchase, and manage land. This gender-sensitive approach not only aligns with international human rights standards but also seeks to empower a significant demographic to contribute meaningfully to economic development and household security.

Environmental sustainability also occupies a prominent place in the policy framework. Ghana's rapid urbanization and expanding agricultural frontiers have led to increasing pressure on land resources, risking degradation and loss of biodiversity. The National Land Policy advocates for land use planning protocols that integrate environmental considerations, encouraging practices that preserve ecosystems and promote sustainable agriculture and development. By coordinating land management with environmental policies, the government envisions mitigating detrimental impacts such as soil erosion, deforestation, and encroachment into protected areas, thereby safeguarding the livelihoods of future generations.

Beyond the national level, Ghana's land policy framework reflects its commitment to international conventions and regional cooperation on land governance issues. The country aligns itself with global initiatives such as the Voluntary Guidelines on the Responsible Governance of Tenure (VGGT) endorsed by the Food and Agriculture Organization (FAO), which stresses transparency, equity, and sustainability in land administration. Ghana's participation in regional bodies, including the Economic Community of West African States (ECOWAS), further promotes the harmonization of land policies across borders, particularly important given the cross-border nature of some land disputes and migratory pressures.

Despite these extensive policy initiatives, the implementation of Ghana's land policy framework has encountered substantial challenges that illustrate the complexity of transforming well-intentioned lofty goals into practical outcomes. One persistent obstacle remains the multiplicity of institutions involved in land management, each with overlapping mandates and sometimes conflicting interests. The Land Commission, Lands Commission's Regional Offices, traditional councils, and municipal authorities often operate in silos, hampering coordinated action and creating windows for corruption and inefficiency. Additionally, the entrenched influence of powerful interest groups and the high stakes associated with valuable urban and peri-urban land continue to spur contentious disputes that test policy resilience.

Moreover, disparities in capacity between urban and rural areas pose significant difficulties in rolling out standardized land registration and governance reforms. While metropolitan areas witness technological advancements such as digital land registries and Geographic Information Systems (GIS) mapping, many rural communities rely on oral agreements and customary protocols that are not fully harmonized with statutory requirements. Bridging this gap demands targeted capacity-building efforts, sensitization campaigns, and the provision of resources to local actors so that land policy measures resonate authentically and operate effectively across diverse contexts.

The government's continuous efforts to pilot innovative land governance projects serve as promising indicators of progress. For instance, the establishment of the Land Governance Support Program (LGSP), supported by international development partners, is a concerted attempt to bolster land tenure security through improved land registration, dispute resolution, and institutional reforms. Similarly, digitization initiatives aim to create a centralized, interoperable database that consolidates land records and facilitates stakeholder access, reducing opportunities for fraud and enhancing transparency. These endeavors embody a forward-looking vision that recognizes technology as an indispensable enabler of sound land policy implementation.

In the realm of conflict prevention, the policy underscores the indispensable role of traditional leaders in safeguarding communal harmony. Traditional authorities, deeply revered in Ghanaian society, maintain custodianship over a substantial portion of the nation's lands, making their engagement essential in any land governance reform. The government's recognition of their pivotal function has translated into efforts to formalize their roles within the statutory land administration system, equipping them with training and legal knowledge that complement their customary authority. This integration aspires to forge a hybrid model of governance that capitalizes on indigenous legitimacy while embedding rule of law principles.

Education and public awareness constitute a foundational pillar of the National Land Policy as well. The policy mandates sustained campaigns to inform citizens about their rights and responsibilities regarding land tenure, registration, and dispute resolution. By empowering communities with knowledge, the policy aims to reduce vulnerabilities exploited by unscrupulous actors and to foster a culture of compliance and respect for land laws. Such educational outreach extends to youth programs, emphasizing the importance of responsible land stewardship for national development.

Finally, the policy framework envisions comprehensive monitoring and evaluation mechanisms designed to track implementation progress and adapt strategies dynamically. Recognizing that land governance is a living process influenced by socio-economic and political changes, these mechanisms facilitate data-driven decision-making and stakeholder feedback loops. Transparency portals and citizen report cards are among the tools proposed to hold officials accountable and measure the efficacy of various interventions.

In essence, Ghana's National Land Policy represents a synthesis of ambitions: to secure land rights for all citizens, harmonize competing tenure systems, prevent and resolve conflicts, and ensure land use that supports sustainable development. It endeavors to harness modern governance tools, legal reforms, community participation, and technological innovations in a concerted effort to tame what has long been a volatile sector prone to disputes and inefficiencies. While the journey towards full realization of these goals remains fraught with institutional and social challenges, the policy framework provides a robust foundation upon which incremental but meaningful transformations continue to unfold for the benefit of Ghana's landowners, investors, and the broader society.

13.2 Institutional Roles in Land Administration

In Ghana, the administration of land is a complex web of institutions, each playing a distinct yet interrelated role in managing the country's most vital resource. The vast tapestry of agencies involved in land governance reflects the nation's multifaceted approach to land management, which melds traditional authority with statutory law, and local community interests with national development priorities. At the heart of this system lies a deliberate effort by the government to streamline land administration, improve transparency, and ultimately prevent the persistent and often debilitating land conflicts that have challenged Ghana's socio-economic landscape for decades.

One of the principal institutions in Ghana's land governance framework is the Land Commission, a statutory body established to coordinate the allocation, management, and administration of public lands on behalf of the government. As the custodian of vested lands – those owned by the state – the Land Commission plays a critical role in ensuring that land is utilized effectively to foster national development. The Commission's responsibilities encompass surveying, mapping, and maintaining land records, which are essential for enabling secure land tenure and facilitating investment. Over the years, recognizing that inadequate land records contribute significantly to disputes, the Land Commission has pursued modernizing these systems through initiatives such as the digitalization of land registries and the creation of integrated land information systems. This shift toward leveraging geospatial technologies and electronic platforms promises to enhance accuracy, reduce bureaucratic delays, and curb fraudulent land dealings that exacerbate conflicts.

Complementing the Land Commission's efforts is the Land Use and Spatial Planning Authority (LUSPA), a relatively newer agency established to oversee spatial planning and land use regulation at national and local levels. Its creation reflects the government's recognition that uncoordinated land development contributes heavily to disputes, especially in rapidly urbanizing centers such as Accra, Kumasi, and Tema. LUSPA's mandate involves designing and enforcing land use plans that balance competing demands – residential, agricultural, industrial, and conservation – in a way that minimizes overlapping claims and promotes sustainable utilization. Beyond planning, the Authority works closely with metropolitan, municipal, and district assemblies to ensure that zoning laws and building regulations are adhered to, thereby preventing unauthorized land acquisitions or construction activities that often ignite conflicts. This institutional check balances investor ambitions with community needs and environmental considerations, integral to proactive conflict prevention.

Equally significant in the land administration ecosystem is the Land Title Registry, a specialized office dedicated to the registration of land titles and interests. Since one of the major root causes of land disputes stems from unclear or contested ownership documentation, the Land Title Registry's role assumes immense importance in providing formal recognition of land rights. The Registry is responsible for issuing titles under the Land Title Registration Law (LTRL), which governs the registration of deeds and titles in Ghana. The implementation of this law is a substantial step towards transitioning from a wholly deed-based system to one that guarantees definitive title ownership, thus shielding landowners from fraudulent claims or duplications. However, the Registry faces persistent challenges, including the backlog of unregistered properties, limited public awareness, and occasional overlapping jurisdictions, all of which impact its effectiveness. To address these hurdles, the government has introduced targeted reforms aiming at decentralizing registration services, extending mobile land registration units to rural areas, and incorporating digital platforms to facilitate easier access and quicker processing times.

At the local government level, the roles of district assemblies and municipal councils are indispensable in the administration of land, particularly as they serve as the immediate regulatory bodies for land transactions, allotments, and dispute mediation within their jurisdictions. These decentralized structures are tasked with the initial approval of land allocations, issuing of building permits, and enforcement of local planning regulations. Their proximity to the grassroots enables them to act swiftly in contentious land disputes, often referring cases to mediation or traditional dispute resolution forums to avoid escalation. Moreover, many of these assemblies have embraced participatory approaches by involving community members in land governance decisions, thereby fostering transparency and enhancing legitimacy. However, challenges of capacity, political interference, and resource constraints sometimes hinder their effective functioning, necessitating continued support from central government institutions.

Traditional authorities remain a pivotal arm within Ghana's land administration, especially given the country's unique dual land tenure system where approximately 80% of land is held under customary tenure. Chiefs and customary councils wield profound influence over land allocation and dispute resolution in their respective areas. Their historical and cultural legitimacy positions them as gatekeepers of customary lands, responsible for granting stool land rights, overseeing family land matters, and arbitrating disputes according to indigenous laws and practices. Recognizing this crucial role, the Ghanaian government has, through various policies and legal frameworks, sought to integrate traditional authority more systematically into formal land administration. The Intended integration also provides an avenue for harnessing their local knowledge and social capital to implement land governance reforms effectively. Training programs have been conducted to enhance the capacity of traditional leaders in record-keeping, transparency, and mediation techniques, bridging the gap between customary practices and statutory requirements.

The Ministry of Lands and Natural Resources serves as the central policy-making body, responsible for formulating and implementing national land policy, coordinating the activities of land administration agencies, and overseeing natural resource management. As the custodian of policy direction, the Ministry garners inputs from diverse stakeholders—including local authorities, traditional leaders, civil society, and private sector actors—to ensure that land reforms align with broader goals of equitable development, environmental sustainability, and economic growth. The policy documents crafted under the Ministry's aegis address key challenges such as land fragmentation, gender inclusivity, and climate change resilience. Importantly, the Ministry spearheads programs aimed at increasing land tenure security, encouraging formalization of customary lands, and fostering investment confidence. These strategic imperatives entail building institutional capacity, promoting legal reforms, and embracing technology-driven solutions across the land sector.

The judicial system, comprising regular courts and specialized bodies such as the Lands and Natural Resources Courts, also plays a crucial role in land administration by adjudicating disputes and enforcing land laws. Courts serve as arbiters for contentious land matters that cannot be settled through mediation or traditional forums. Their decisions set legal precedents that clarify ambiguities in tenure and ownership, offering a framework of predictability and rule of law. However, the judiciary often grapples with delays, procedural complexities, and limited expertise in customary land issues, which can exacerbate grievances or deter parties from seeking formal remedies. To counter these challenges, judicial reforms have aimed at establishing specialized divisions with trained judges equipped to handle land disputes expeditiously and fairly. Efforts to improve access to justice include legal aid services for marginalized groups and public education campaigns about judicial processes.

Parallel to the courts, alternative dispute resolution (ADR) mechanisms have gained considerable prominence as institutional tools for resolving land conflicts more amicably and efficiently. Government agencies have promoted ADR approaches such as mediation, arbitration, and negotiation clinics, often in partnership with civil society organizations and traditional authorities. These mechanisms emphasize dialogue, consensus-building, and respect for local customs, which frequently lead to more sustainable conflict outcomes. To institutionalize ADR, policies mandate the inclusion of mediation options prior to court proceedings, and training programs have been conducted to develop professional mediators specialized in land conflicts. The integration of ADR within the formal land administration system helps to alleviate the burden on courts, shorten dispute resolution timelines, and restore community relations fractured by land disagreements.

Complementing institutional reforms are various government-led initiatives aimed explicitly at improving land governance and curtailing conflicts. Programs such as the Ghana Land Administration Project (LAP), supported by international development partners, illustrate the commitment to modernizing land administration processes through capacity-building, system upgrades, and policy alignment. The LAP, for instance, focuses on strengthening institutional coordination, improving land registration coverage, and raising public awareness about land rights and responsibilities. Such initiatives also underscore the importance of citizen engagement, empowering communities with information to assert their land claims and participate in decision-making. The government's push for transparency extends to creating public access portals where stakeholders can verify land ownership data and transaction histories, thereby deterring fraudulent practices and fostering trust.

Technological advancements have caused a seismic shift in the practices of land administration agencies. The adoption of Geographic Information Systems (GIS), aerial drones for mapping, and blockchain for secure transactions demonstrates the government's strategic vision to harness innovation to resolve longstanding land governance inefficiencies. These technologies offer unprecedented accuracy in mapping land parcels, tracking ownership changes, and enabling real-time conflict monitoring. Additionally, mobile applications and electronic platforms facilitate easier registration, payment of fees, and submission of dispute complaints, making land services more accessible, especially to rural populations. The intersection of technology with institutional frameworks signifies a move toward a more transparent, accountable, and efficient system, which is pivotal in reducing the incidence and intensity of land conflicts.

At the same time, the government has recognized that institutional roles cannot operate in silos if they are to effectively mitigate land conflicts. Inter-agency collaboration and coordination mechanisms have thus been institutionalized, ensuring that land administration bodies share information, harmonize regulations, and jointly address contentious issues. Policy forums, joint committees, and integrated databases enable a cohesive regulatory environment where overlapping mandates are minimized, and enforcement is consistent. Such synergies are crucial in managing the complex intersections of urban development, customary land tenure, environmental concerns, and commercial investments. Furthermore, partnerships with non-governmental organizations, academic institutions, and international bodies bring expertise, funding, and legitimacy to these multi-stakeholder governance efforts.

Despite these significant strides, gaps remain that challenge the full realization of effective land governance through institutional roles. Issues such as corruption, political interference, inadequate funding, and limitations in technical capacity continue to plague some agencies, undermining public confidence and restraining performance. The proliferation of conflicting laws and unclear delineation of authority sometimes leads to jurisdictional tussles, which in turn fuel disputes rather than quelling them. Moreover, the underrepresentation of vulnerable groups—especially women, youth, and informal settlers—in institutional decision-making constrains the inclusiveness and equity of land administration outcomes. Nevertheless, ongoing reforms, legal reviews, and capacity enhancement efforts signal a proactive governmental stance toward addressing these gaps systematically.

In conclusion, the institutional framework governing land administration in Ghana is a dynamic and evolving network of government agencies, traditional authorities, judicial bodies, and other stakeholders, each with specialized roles yet collectively charged with ensuring that land serves as a foundation for peace, prosperity, and sustainability. Government initiatives aimed at improving land governance, registration, and conflict prevention increasingly emphasize modern technology, inter-institutional coordination, community involvement, and legal reforms. While challenges abound, the commitment to continuous improvement reflects an understanding that robust, transparent, and fair institutional roles are indispensable in safeguarding land rights, resolving disputes, and unlocking the full potential of Ghana's land resources for national development.

13.3 Reform Measures and Their Impact

In recent years, Ghana has witnessed a remarkable wave of reform initiatives aimed at restructuring and strengthening land governance systems, a response necessitated by the escalating prevalence and complexity of land conflicts that threaten social stability, economic development, and environmental sustainability. The government's commitment to overhauling land administration began with the recognition that ineffective management, bureaucratic inefficiency, lack of transparency, and the dissonance between customary and statutory systems were at the heart of the persistent disputes that erupted sporadically across urban and rural landscapes alike. As such, reform measures have primarily gravitated towards enhancing land registration processes, modernizing land information systems, clarifying land tenure security, and fostering preventative mechanisms that mitigate conflicts before they crystallize into intractable disputes. These reforms, while ambitious, are deeply intertwined with both the nation's historical legacies and contemporary socio-political dynamics, making their assessment a nuanced endeavor.

One of the most noteworthy government-led efforts in recent times has been the digitization and modernization of the land registration system, spearheaded by the Land Commission and supported by various development partners. This digital transformation aims to replace the often fragmented, paper-based, and highly localized methods with a centralized, accessible, and user-friendly platform capable of streamlining land title registration and verification. By embedding geographic information systems (GIS) into the registration process, the reforms intend to facilitate precise mapping of land parcels, reduce overlap and ambiguities in land boundaries, and expedite transactions. These technological advancements promise not only operational efficiency but also the curb of corrupt practices that have previously crept into land dealings via opacity and discretionary manipulation. The introduction of a digital registry is expected to bring about greater tenure security, particularly for marginalized groups whose interests are frequently overlooked in traditional land dealings. Nonetheless, the roll-out of this digital framework has faced significant challenges, including insufficient infrastructural investment in rural areas, limited technological literacy among intended users, and bureaucratic inertia. Furthermore, the sensitive and at times volatile nature of land ownership disputes complicates efforts to create inclusive databases, as stakeholders harbor mistrust of formalized records that may curtail customary rights or newly claimed entitlements.

In parallel with technological reforms, legislative initiatives have sought to reconcile the coexistence of customary and statutory land tenure systems. Ghana's pluralistic land tenure structure—where customary ownership governs about 80% of the land, while statutory laws dominate formal urban and commercial arrangements—has generated persistent tensions. Government reforms have attempted to codify certain customary practices within the statutory framework to provide clearer legal recognition while preserving cultural nuances. For instance, amendments to laws governing stool lands and the authority of traditional leaders have aimed to delineate responsibilities in land allocation, dispute resolution, and stewardship. This delicate balance endeavours to respect the revered traditional institutions that command legitimacy and authority at the community level, while imposing accountability mechanisms aligned with rule of law principles. Despite the careful legal drafting, challenges persist as many customary authorities remain ambivalent or resistant, perceiving statutory encroachment as threats to their autonomy. Consequently, the implementation phase has often been hampered by inconsistent enforcement, jurisdictional overlap, and conflicting interpretations between community elders and government officials.

Another core aspect of reform revolves around conflict prevention and resolution strategies embedded within land governance. Recognizing that land disputes often flourish in the absence of early warning systems and community engagement, government policies have incorporated mechanisms to facilitate dialogue, mediation, and participatory land-use planning. Efforts to institutionalize Alternative Dispute Resolution (ADR) approaches, such as mediation committees complementing court processes, have gained traction. These local ADR frameworks are designed to be culturally sensitive, accessible, and quicker than formal judicial procedures, which are frequently congested, costly, and intimidating for ordinary citizens. The promotion of community land forums and stakeholder consultations further exemplify government attempts to nurture social cohesion around land management decisions. These initiatives have yielded pockets of success in curbing the escalation of disputes and fostering mutual understanding among contending parties. Yet, scaling these practices requires consistent funding, capacity-building for mediators, and the political will to integrate traditional conflict resolution methods with formal legal standards. The historical lack of trust between government agents and local communities sometimes undermines these engagement efforts, particularly in regions where grievances against land dispossession have accumulated over generations.

Perhaps one of the most ambitious yet contentious reforms has been attempts at comprehensive land policy formulation designed to harmonize existing statutes, streamline land administration agencies, and develop sustainable frameworks for land use and development control. The policy discourse emphasizes decentralization, aiming to bring land management decisions closer to the grassroots while enhancing accountability and transparency. This approach foregrounds principles such as equitable land access, environmental stewardship, gender inclusivity, and economic viability, reflecting an integrative philosophy toward land governance. Legislative efforts to consolidate land institutions, like merging the various land-related agencies, are intended to eliminate duplication, reduce administrative bottlenecks, and present a coherent front to the public. Moreover, reforms prioritize the revision of land leasehold regimes, property tax systems, and urban planning regulations to align with contemporary economic realities and investment trends. However, the institutional restructuring encounters resistance from entrenched bureaucracies and vested interests that benefit from the status quo. Policy inconsistency and political interference periodically stall reform momentum, creating uncertainty for investors and communities alike.

The impact of reform measures must also be understood against the backdrop of Ghana's rapidly urbanizing society and evolving socio-economic landscape. Urban expansion pressures demand swift and reliable land management systems capable of coping with increasing demand for residential, commercial, and industrial land. Government initiatives have consequently had to adopt a forward-looking perspective, embedding strategic land-use planning and zoning controls within the reform architecture. The creation of urban land information systems, integrated with municipal planning departments, represents tangible steps towards addressing the challenges of informal settlements and speculative land grabbing. Nevertheless, the speed of urban growth often outpaces institutional responses, leaving gaps where conflicts emerge from ambiguous land claims, forced evictions, and inadequate compensation. Thus, while reforms exhibit a pragmatic orientation towards urban realities, their execution is frequently reactive rather than anticipatory, necessitating continuous refinement and investment.

Critically, the socio-cultural dimension of land reforms cannot be overstated. Land in Ghana embodies more than mere property rights; it is deeply woven into identity, tradition, and communal survival. Government reform approaches that inadequately appreciate these cultural attachments risk engendering alienation and resistance. To counter this, several initiatives have promoted inclusive stakeholder consultations during policy development and reform rollout phases. Engagement with traditional leaders, community members, and civil society organizations is increasingly viewed as essential to validate reforms and integrate indigenous knowledge and customs. Additionally, efforts to afford women and vulnerable groups better participation and representation in land governance have emerged as important milestones. Where reforms have succeeded in fostering inclusive dialogues, they have laid foundations for sustainable acceptance and legitimacy. Conversely, reforms perceived as top-down impositions or favoring elite interests exacerbate social fractures and complicate conflict prevention.

Despite these ongoing efforts, substantial challenges remain that temper the overall impact of reform measures. One persistent issue lies in capacity deficits at local government levels responsible for implementing land policies and managing registrations. Many district assemblies lack the technical expertise, human resources, and financial means to operationalize new systems and effectively enforce regulations. This shortfall undermines the practical realization of reforms on the ground and fuels perceptions of inefficiency and inconsistency. Corruption, too, continues to plague land administration processes, with fraudulent documentation, bribery, and patronage networks compromising public trust. The reform drive has grappled with devising punitive mechanisms and incentive structures to deter malpractice without alienating essential personnel.

Legal system bottlenecks present another formidable obstacle. Courts remain overburdened with land-related cases, and adjudication processes can span years, eroding confidence in statutory remedies. The duality and overlap between customary and formal legal regimes contribute to jurisdictional confusion and forum shopping by disputants. Efforts to harmonize laws and streamline procedures face slow legislative and judicial adaptation. Moreover, emerging land conflicts increasingly encompass environmental concerns, climate change impacts, and resource scarcity, introducing new dimensions that current reforms have only begun to address.

The political economy surrounding land governance intricately shapes the trajectory of reforms. Land in Ghana represents a lucrative asset class, attracting commercial developers, agriculture investors, and speculative actors. Pressure from these stakeholders often influences policy choices and implementation priorities, sometimes at odds with local communities' needs and rights. Navigating these tensions demands political deftness and genuine commitment to equitable land distribution, which can be challenging in a context where patronage and political capital intertwine with land allocation decisions. Consequently, reforms risk being undermined if they fail to insulate land governance from politicization and ensure transparent, merit-based processes.

In reflecting on the impact of reform measures to date, it is evident that progress, while significant, is uneven and fraught with complexities. Improved land registration systems have enhanced record-keeping and transactional clarity in accessible areas but remain out of reach for many rural citizens. Legislative clarifications have provided a framework for coexistence between customary and formal land authorities but practical enforcement and collaboration lag. Conflict prevention strategies have fostered early interventions and grassroots dialogues in various localities, though replicability and sustainability require bolstered resources and institutional integration. Policy and institutional restructuring have laid conceptual foundations for coherent land governance but continue to wrestle with bureaucratic resistance, vested interests, and political interference. The socio-cultural integration of reforms is promising but necessitates ongoing commitment to inclusivity and sensitization.

Looking ahead, the challenge for Ghana lies in consolidating reform gains through sustained investment in capacity-building, technological infrastructure, and public education. Bridging the rural-urban divide in access to land services, enhancing transparency and accountability mechanisms, and deepening partnerships among government, traditional authorities, and civil society constitute essential next steps. Innovating legal frameworks to address emerging land governance issues, including environmental sustainability and climate resilience, will be vital. Most importantly, a holistic approach that acknowledges the complex interplay of history, culture, economics, and politics in land matters is indispensable for reforms to deliver transformative impact and contribute meaningfully to the resolution of land conflicts across Ghana.

CHAPTER 14

COMMUNITY PARTICIPATION AND AWARENESS

14.1 Community Engagement Strategies

Engaging communities effectively in land governance is an essential pivot around which sustainable conflict resolution and equitable land management revolve. The notion of community engagement goes far beyond a mere procedural obligation; it embodies a genuine process of partnership-building that respects local knowledge, cultures, and aspirations. In Ghana, where land is deeply intertwined with identity, tradition, and economic survival, strategies for involving people in land matters must be deeply nuanced and culturally sensitive, fostering an environment in which citizens feel heard, informed, and empowered to influence land-related decisions that affect their lives. One cannot overstate the importance of education within these engagement frameworks. Educating citizens about their land rights, the legal frameworks governing land ownership, the roles of various institutions, and the pathways for recourse in cases of disputes is fundamental. Often, lack of awareness or misinformation exacerbates misunderstandings and fuels conflicts. Therefore, community education initiatives must be designed to be accessible, inclusive, and context-specific, employing local languages and formats that resonate with the audiences' lived realities.

A crucial approach to community education involves participatory workshops and fora, where government officials, traditional leaders, legal experts, and community members convene to discuss land issues openly and collectively. Unlike top-down messaging, these forums encourage dialogue, question-and-answer sessions, and shared experiences, which validate community perspectives and foster a sense of collective ownership over land governance processes. Additionally, visual aids such as maps, diagrams, and storytelling enhance comprehension and engagement, especially in rural areas where literacy levels may vary. Complementing these face-to-face engagements are innovative outreach campaigns leveraging radio programs, community theatre, and mobile technology. Radio remains one of the most effective and wide-reaching channels in Ghana, capable of penetrating remote communities and sparking public conversations on land matters. Community theatre, on the other hand, taps into Ghana's rich oral traditions and dramatizes land issues in relatable, emotive narratives that resonate with both young and old. Meanwhile, the burgeoning use of mobile phones for SMS-based alerts and interactive platforms allows timely dissemination of information and enables communities to report land disputes or suspicious activities swiftly, thereby preventing escalation.

Promoting transparency within land governance structures is another pillar critical to strengthening community trust and participation. Transparency is essential in dispelling suspicions of corruption, manipulation, or exclusion that have historically plagued land administration in Ghana. To this end, government agencies and traditional authorities must adopt clear, open procedures for land transactions, dispute resolutions, and record-keeping. The establishment of public land registries that are accessible to communities reinforces this aim, demystifying the ownership status of parcels of land and clarifying legal boundaries. By integrating technological solutions such as Geographic Information Systems (GIS) and digitized land records, transparency is further enhanced, as discrepancies, overlaps, or irregularities become more visible and easier to rectify. This technological infusion also helps to democratize land data, making it possible for ordinary citizens, not just elites or speculators, to verify claims and contest dubious assertions. However, transparency cannot be fully realized without accountability. Public hearings, consultative meetings, and grievance redress mechanisms embedded within land governance allow community members to hold custodians of land responsible and demand explanations. More so, involving civil society organizations and independent monitors in oversight roles ensures that transparency leads to tangible improvements rather than merely symbolic gestures.

Empowering communities involves building their capacity not only to understand their rights and responsibilities but also to assert them effectively in decision-making processes. This empowerment begins with recognizing traditional structures and community leadership, which have long governed land use through customary laws and practices. Chiefs, elders, and clan heads hold significant influence and legitimacy, making their involvement in engagement strategies indispensable. However, empowerment also requires challenging undemocratic practices within these traditional institutions, advocating for gender inclusivity, youth participation, and equitable representation. Initiatives that train community leaders on land governance principles, negotiation skills, and conflict mediation can transform them into proactive agents of peace and development rather than sources of discord or gatekeepers of information. At the grassroots, the establishment of land rights committees or local resource management groups serves to decentralize decision-making and bring it closer to the people affected by those decisions. These groups can act as first responders to emerging conflicts, facilitate dialogue, and liaise with formal institutions to expedite resolutions.

Moreover, economic empowerment plays a significant role in equipping communities to engage robustly in land matters. Land conflicts often arise when marginalized groups feel dispossessed or threatened by commercial interests. Providing alternative livelihood opportunities, access to credit, and technical support in agriculture or small-scale enterprises can reduce the vulnerabilities that make communities susceptible to exploitation and displacement. Such socio-economic interventions also create incentives for communities to invest in sustainable land management and stewardship, generating a virtuous cycle where engagement begets responsibility, which in turn fosters stability. Grassroots empowerment is further strengthened by ensuring that citizens have platforms to participate in policymaking processes at district, regional, and national levels. Mechanisms such as town hall meetings, public consultations, and inclusion in land reform committees grant communities voices that can influence legislative frameworks and their enforcement. This integration bridges the often-observed gap between policy formulation and grassroots realities, preventing top-down approaches that alienate the very people they intend to serve.

An essential dimension of community engagement in land governance is recognizing and accommodating the diverse voices and interests within communities. Land is not a monolithic asset; it intersects with gender, age, class, and ethnicity, producing multiple and sometimes competing claims. Women, in particular, face systemic barriers in land access and ownership due to cultural norms and legal constraints, often rendering them invisible in land discussions. Effective engagement strategies must, therefore, incorporate gender-sensitive approaches that actively empower women to participate and assert land rights. This can be achieved through women-focused forums, legal aid clinics specializing in women's land issues, and advocacy campaigns aimed at shifting social attitudes. Youth engagement is equally critical, as the younger generation holds the key to future land stewardship and stability. Empowering youth through education, mentorship, and inclusion in land governance bodies can curtail intergenerational conflicts and promote innovative ideas for land use and conservation.

In the face of rapid urbanization and land commercialization in Ghana, bridging rural and urban perspectives on land becomes imperative. Urban dwellers, investors, and developers introduce new dynamics that can either conflict with or complement traditional land uses. Therefore, engagement strategies must encourage dialogue across these divides, fostering mutual understanding and collaboration. Multi-stakeholder platforms that include government officials, traditional authorities, private investors, and civil society can serve as incubators for negotiated agreements that respect community rights while accommodating economic development. These platforms can also pilot participatory land use planning exercises, where community inputs guide zoning, resettlement, or infrastructure projects, ensuring that development does not come at the unjust expense of marginalized groups.

Lastly, sustainability in community engagement hinges on long-term commitment and adaptability. Land governance is an evolving landscape, influenced by policy shifts, environmental changes, market forces, and demographic trends. Engagement strategies must be flexible, continuously assessing the effectiveness of participatory processes and incorporating feedback to refine approaches. Capacity-building for communities should be ongoing, not one-off events, fostering resilience and self-reliance in navigating future land challenges. Governments and development partners should invest in institutionalizing community engagement within their organizational mandates, allocating resources and personnel dedicated to maintaining open lines of communication and support with communities. In this way, the relationship between the people and the custodians of land management becomes a living partnership that nurtures trust, transparency, and shared responsibility.

In sum, community engagement in land matters in Ghana is a multifaceted endeavor requiring comprehensive strategies that educate, promote transparency, and empower citizens. It demands the integration of traditional wisdom with modern governance approaches, the harnessing of technology alongside cultural expression, and the equitable inclusion of all societal segments, especially marginalized groups. When citizens are genuinely engaged, they transcend the role of passive subjects to become active stakeholders shaping the destiny of their land. This transformation is essential for resolving conflicts, preventing future disputes, and ensuring that land, as a vital resource, contributes sustainably to Ghana's social cohesion, economic development, and national prosperity.

14.2 Public Education Campaigns

In the complex landscape of land governance in Ghana, public education campaigns play an indispensable role in demystifying land rights and laws for the broader population. These campaigns are not merely auxiliary measures; they form the bedrock upon which transparent, inclusive, and effective land management can be constructed. A well-informed citizenry is empowered to recognize their rights, understand legal processes, and engage meaningfully in land-related decisions that affect their lives. This empowerment, in turn, contributes to reducing conflicts, fostering social cohesion, and promoting equitable development. Therefore, an essential component of resolving and preventing land disputes lies in comprehensive, sustained, and culturally sensitive public education initiatives tailored to diverse Ghanaian communities.

At a fundamental level, public education campaigns aim to translate the often complex and jargon-laden legal language surrounding land ownership, tenure systems, and dispute resolution into accessible, relatable information. Ghana's dual system of land administration—where customary ownership intertwines with statutory law—poses challenges for many citizens, especially those in rural areas with limited formal education or access to legal expertise. Many individuals and communities remain unaware of their legal rights or the procedures required to secure land titles, leading to vulnerability to exploitation or inadvertent conflicts. Mandatory awareness efforts must therefore prioritize clarity, simplicity, and cultural resonance. Using local languages, narratives, folk stories, and analogies that reflect indigenous values helps bridge the gap between abstract legal constructs and lived realities. Public education that resonates with local customs is more likely to inspire trust and prompt proactive engagement, rather than apathy or resistance.

The strategic design of these campaigns often involves multiple platforms and media to maximize reach and impact. Traditional communication channels like community durbars, town hall meetings, and local radio programs continue to be instrumental in rural Ghana. Community leaders and chiefs play pivotal roles in endorsing such gatherings, lending legitimacy and attracting participation. These events provide an interactive space for dialogue, where citizens can ask questions, share concerns, and receive immediate clarification. Incorporating drama, storytelling, and folk music in community gatherings enhances receptiveness, especially among illiterate populations, by embedding lessons within culturally familiar forms of knowledge transmission. In more urbanized or semi-urban areas, print media, social media, and mobile technology applications are increasingly used to disseminate information rapidly and widely. Partnerships with popular media personalities or influencers who command respect and attention offer innovative avenues to engage younger demographics and urban dwellers, expanding the educational reach beyond traditional confines.

A critical objective of public education campaigns is to foster transparency within the land administration system. Transparency deficiencies—such as opaque transaction processes, corruption, and insufficient record-keeping—are significant drivers of mistrust and disputes. Education initiatives must familiarize citizens with the official procedures for registering land, transferring ownership, resolving disputes, and accessing government services. This knowledge equips individuals to navigate bureaucratic processes more confidently and recognize irregularities or malpractices. Beyond technical know-how, campaigns should institutionalize concepts of accountability and civic responsibility, encouraging communities to demand openness from authorities and participate actively in monitoring land governance practices. Encouraging transparency not only prevents land conflicts but also cultivates good governance and strengthens democratic institutions at the grassroots level.

Community empowerment underpins the transformative potential of public education campaigns. Beyond raising awareness, effective initiatives instill a sense of agency, enabling communities to become active stakeholders rather than passive recipients of top-down policies. Participatory approaches to education ensure that community voices are heard and incorporated, affirming their knowledge about land and enhancing the legitimacy of the information disseminated. For example, training local facilitators—trusted community members who act as relay agents of land information—ensures continuity of knowledge and nurtures local leadership networks. Such facilitators can help demystify legal jargon, mediate preliminary disputes, and guide community members through complex land administration processes, thereby building institutional capacity from within. These grassroots linkages foster self-reliance in land governance and reduce overdependence on external authorities, which is often a bottleneck in resolving disputes swiftly and fairly.

Moreover, public education campaigns must address the gendered dimensions of land access and ownership that have historically marginalized women in Ghanaian society. Discriminatory customs and incomplete legal enforcement frequently deprive women of equitable land rights, leading to conflicts and social inequities. Education programs centered on gender sensitivity and women's land rights challenge entrenched patriarchal norms and promote inclusive decision-making frameworks. Empowering women with knowledge of their entitlements and procedural rights not only advances social justice but also diversifies community leadership in land management, contributing to more balanced conflict resolution. Collaborative partnerships with women's organizations, faith groups, and grassroots associations enhance the resonance and reach of gender-focused education, ensuring culturally appropriate messaging and community acceptance.

The design and execution of public education campaigns also increasingly leverage technological innovations to overcome traditional barriers. The proliferation of mobile phones in Ghana presents immense opportunities for disseminating land education content through SMS alerts, interactive voice response systems, and mobile apps that provide legal information, report disputes, or schedule appointments with land officials. These tools increase convenience and broaden accessibility, especially for remote or marginalized populations. Furthermore, digital platforms enable the aggregation of feedback and real-time monitoring of campaign efficacy, allowing for adaptive strategy refinement. Online portals that visualize land boundaries and tenure maps enhance transparency and communal understanding. However, the digital divide remains a challenge; hence hybrid models combining digital and face-to-face engagements are necessary to ensure inclusivity and bridge knowledge gaps.

Sustainability and impact measurement are vital considerations in public education efforts. Short-term awareness drives, while useful, often lack the depth and continuity required to effect lasting behavioral change and cultural shift. Campaigns integrated into the broader framework of national land policies, community development programs, and educational curricula tend to have deeper penetration and ongoing influence. For example, embedding land rights education in schools and adult literacy classes ensures that future generations grow up with an inherent understanding of land governance principles. Similarly, periodic refresher sessions within communities help reinforce messages and update citizens on legislative changes or emerging challenges. Rigorous monitoring and evaluation mechanisms that track knowledge uptake, attitude shifts, and reduction in land-related disputes provide evidence for policy refinement and resource allocation, enhancing future campaign design.

In essence, public education campaigns form the connective tissue that binds the multiplicity of actors engaged in Ghana's land governance challenge. By actively informing citizens about their rights, the nuances of land laws, and available avenues for recourse, these campaigns mitigate misunderstanding and misinformation—the very seeds of conflict. Their success hinges upon culturally attuned approaches, inclusive participation, gender sensitivity, technological innovation, and sustained commitment. When harmonized with transparent land administration and community empowerment, public education becomes a formidable instrument in transforming land from a source of strife into a foundation of stability, prosperity, and social justice across Ghana's diverse landscapes. It beckons a future in which every Ghanaian, irrespective of location or status, can confidently assert their land rights and contribute to a harmonious national tapestry woven through mutual respect and shared responsibility.

14.3 Empowerment and Capacity Building

The empowerment of communities and the enhancement of their capacity to engage effectively in land governance stand as pivotal strategies in addressing the deep-rooted conflicts that have long plagued the management of land resources in Ghana. Given the complex interplay of customary practices and statutory laws, as well as the myriad socio-economic pressures that exacerbate land disputes, it becomes imperative to develop approaches that go beyond mere regulation or adjudication. Instead, true progress requires cultivating an informed and confident citizenry, equipped with the necessary knowledge, skills, and tools to participate meaningfully in land-related decisions. This approach not only fosters ownership and respect for communal and individual rights but also nurtures transparency and accountability within the broader framework of land administration.

At the heart of empowerment lies education, a multifaceted process that must address the diverse audiences involved in land matters—from traditional authorities and local community members to government officials and legal practitioners. For communities, particularly in rural areas where customary tenure dominates, there is often a considerable gap in understanding the nuances of statutory land laws, formal registration processes, and the legal implications of land transactions. Bridging these gaps demands targeted training programs that are both contextually relevant and sensitive to cultural perceptions of land ownership. Educational initiatives should therefore be designed not as top-down impositions but as participatory dialogues, where local knowledge and customary norms are recognized and integrated alongside formal legal principles. This inclusive pedagogy enhances receptivity and encourages community members to see themselves as active agents rather than passive subjects within the land governance ecosystem.

Moreover, empowering communities eclectically involves equipping them with practical tools to engage transparently with land administration processes. Access to accurate information—whether about land boundaries, ownership claims, or governmental policies—remains a fundamental challenge in many parts of Ghana. Historically, opaque record-keeping systems and bureaucratic inertia have created breeding grounds for land conflicts, feeding mistrust and misinformation. To counter this, capacity-building initiatives must prioritize the development and deployment of user-friendly platforms that facilitate real-time access to land data. Technological innovations such as Geographic Information Systems (GIS), mobile applications for land registration, and public dashboards can democratize information, enabling citizens to verify claims, report irregularities, and track the status of land transactions without undue dependence on intermediaries. Training community representatives and traditional authorities on the use of such technologies further deepens transparency and fosters confidence in the management of shared resources.

In tandem with knowledge and technology, empowerment also involves nurturing the institutional capacity within local governance structures. Chiefs, elders, land committee members, and other customary custodians frequently serve as the first point of contact in land disputes. However, without adequate training on human rights, alternative dispute resolution mechanisms, and the evolving statutory framework, these traditional leaders may inadvertently perpetuate injustices or exacerbate conflicts. Organized workshops, seminars, and continuous professional development programs tailored for these actors can enhance their understanding and improve their competencies in adjudicating claims fairly, mediating disputes, and collaborating effectively with formal institutions. Importantly, such capacity building should also encourage inclusivity by promoting the participation of marginalized groups—women, youth, and minority communities—whose voices are often sidelined in land matters, despite their significant stakes and contributions.

Complementing formal capacity development efforts, peer learning and knowledge exchange can serve as powerful avenues for empowerment. Communities that have successfully navigated land conflicts or implemented innovative governance practices can share experiences and lessons learned with others facing similar challenges. Creating platforms for such exchanges—whether through regional forums, community visits, or digital networks—injects local realism into theoretical knowledge and inspires adaptive solutions rooted in indigenous contexts. Moreover, these interactions dilute the myth of isolated struggles, forging solidarity among diverse groups and stimulating collective action toward equitable land management. This collaborative spirit also opens opportunities for cross-sectoral partnerships, drawing together civil society organizations, academic institutions, and government agencies to coalesce around shared goals.

Public education campaigns further reinforce empowerment by raising awareness about citizens' land rights and responsibilities. These campaigns should employ multiple communication channels, including radio broadcasts, community theater, storytelling, social media, and printed materials in local languages, to ensure wide reach and resonance. Emphasizing the importance of land tenure security, lawful acquisition, and dispute prevention, such outreach can shift attitudes and behaviors over time, reducing incidences of fraudulent sales, illegal encroachments, and land grabbing. By demystifying land laws and dispelling misconceptions, public education also creates an enabling environment where ordinary Ghanaians feel encouraged to seek legal assistance and engage with land administration authorities rather than resort to informal or violent methods.

Transparency, a cornerstone for peaceful land governance, is inextricably linked to empowerment. Empowered communities are not only better equipped to understand land issues but also more effective in demanding accountability from trustees, administrators, and policymakers. When citizens can participate openly in decision-making forums, hold leaders accountable through advocacy or litigation, and monitor the performance of land institutions, the likelihood of corruption and malfeasance diminishes significantly. This shift requires reforms that institutionalize public participation, including the establishment of accessible complaint mechanisms, citizen advisory boards, and open hearings on land-related policies. Training community members to organize themselves, engage constructively with authorities, and articulate concerns diplomatically is essential to tapping the full potential of participatory governance.

Capacity building in land governance also inevitably must contend with the realities of urbanization and rapid demographic change. As cities expand and rural populations increasingly migrate to peri-urban areas, new forms of tenure arrangements and complex land markets emerge. Communities caught in this dynamic often find themselves vulnerable to exploitation, unable to navigate the intricacies of land sales, mortgages, or development plans. Here, empowerment translates into equipping residents with specialized knowledge about their rights in urban contexts, understanding zoning laws, negotiating fair compensations during land acquisitions, and recognizing mechanisms for appeal and recourse. Training municipal officials and urban planners concurrently ensures that their approaches are inclusive, culturally sensitive, and grounded in principles of fairness and sustainability.

One cannot overstate the importance of fostering a mindset of self-reliance and proactive stewardship among community members. Empowerment and capacity building must encourage not only awareness and skills but also a sense of responsibility toward managing communal lands sustainably. This involves educating people on environmental conservation, equitable land use planning, and the long-term implications of land degradation or unsound development. By linking land governance to broader developmental aspirations such as food security, climate resilience, and poverty reduction, communities are motivated to balance competing interests and prioritize the collective good. In practical terms, capacity-building programs might integrate modules on agroforestry, sustainable farming practices, or community-based natural resource management, thereby equipping citizens with the tools to align their economic activities with stewardship obligations.

Financial literacy stands as another critical dimension of empowerment, particularly given the increase in commercial interests and land transactions that demand contractual understanding and fiscal prudence. Many community members often enter land markets without adequate preparation to evaluate prices, assess risks, or navigate loan agreements. Hence, training in financial planning, contract law basics, and negotiation tactics equips them to make informed decisions and avoid exploitation. Furthermore, such knowledge enables communities to engage on equal footing with investors and developers, ensuring that land deals yield fair benefits and respect social and environmental safeguards.

Behind every effective capacity-building endeavor is the recognition that empowerment is a gradual, context-sensitive process that must be sustained over time. One-off workshops or sporadic training sessions fall short in delivering lasting change. Instead, continuous engagement, follow-up support, mentorship, and refresher courses are essential to reinforce learning, adapt to evolving challenges, and deepen community confidence. The creation of community resource centers or knowledge hubs can serve as focal points for ongoing education, legal aid, and mediation services. In resource-constrained settings, leveraging partnerships with nongovernmental organizations, academic institutions, and donor agencies can provide critical technical and financial support to sustain these initiatives.

At the policy level, an enabling environment that prioritizes empowerment and capacity building signals commitment to inclusive land governance. Governments must allocate dedicated budgets, streamline institutional mandates, and establish monitoring frameworks that track the effectiveness of training programs and community participation. Policies that institutionalize mechanisms for integrating customary norms with statutory requirements often include provisions for capacity enhancement of traditional authorities and community representatives. This structural support facilitates a symbiotic relationship between formal systems and grassroots actors, dissolving historical tensions and creating pathways for co-management of land resources.

In practice, some areas in Ghana have already begun to demonstrate how empowerment and capacity building can transform land governance. For example, the involvement of youth groups in mapping customary lands with support from technology firms has fostered greater clarity in land boundaries and reduced inter-family disputes. Similarly, collaborations between local governments and universities in organizing land literacy campaigns have improved public knowledge and encouraged timely registration of land parcels. Such successes highlight the importance of adaptive, locally anchored approaches that respect the diversity of Ghana's land tenure arrangements while fostering a culture of transparency and dialogue.

Ultimately, empowering communities and building their capacity in land governance is not merely a tool for conflict resolution; it is a transformative strategy that redefines how land is valued, governed, and shared. By arming citizens with knowledge, fostering transparency, nurturing inclusive institutions, and encouraging proactive stewardship, Ghana can harness the power of its people to ensure that land fulfills its potential as a source of identity, livelihood, and sustainable development. In the face of growing population pressures and economic demands, this holistic empowerment approach offers a beacon of hope, demonstrating that lasting peace and prosperity are achievable when communities are entrusted with the skills and agency to safeguard their most precious resource.

CHAPTER 15

TECHNOLOGY AND LAND CONFLICT RESOLUTION

15.1 Digital Land Registries

The notion of digital land registries carries with it an air of transformative potential, especially in a country like Ghana where land disputes are deeply entrenched in the socio-economic and cultural fabric of society. At its core, the implementation of digital records represents a fundamental shift from traditional, often cumbersome and paper-based systems to a more streamlined, transparent, and accessible framework for land management. This transition is neither merely technical nor mechanistic; it is profoundly intertwined with the dynamics of governance, justice, and community trust. Digital land registries, bolstered by Geographic Information Systems (GIS), mobile applications, and other technological innovations, hold the promise of recalibrating the power structures that have long shaped land tenure, ownership, and conflict in Ghana.

To understand the profound implications of digital land registries in the Ghanaian context, one must consider the historic and operational weaknesses of the existing land administration system. Traditionally, land records in Ghana have been fragmented, inconsistently maintained, and vulnerable to loss or destruction. Paper-based documents, scattered across various government departments and sometimes in the custody of traditional authorities, create bottlenecks in access, verification, and dispute adjudication. The opacity of paper records opens a fertile ground for fraudulent transactions, multiple claims to the same parcel, and opaque negotiations. In rural settings, customary land tenure systems, with their oral traditions and community-based validations, often do not align neatly with the statutory, written frameworks that digital registries seek to standardize. This layered complexity presents both a challenge and an opportunity for digital systems.

The integration of Geographic Information Systems (GIS) into land management marks a monumental leap forward because it enables the visualization and precise analysis of land parcels in spatial terms. GIS technology encapsulates not only the boundaries of land plots, but also their topographical features, neighboring plots, infrastructures, and sometimes even sociodemographic details of occupants or users. By digitizing land surveys and embedding them in a centralized system, GIS diminishes the ambiguity that has historically fueled disputes—uncertain boundaries are clarified through satellite imagery and cartographic overlays that can be updated continuously and made publicly accessible. In Ghana, pilot programs and burgeoning efforts by government agencies, such as the Land Commission, to harness GIS have demonstrated its immense utility in converting vague and contested lands into distinctly mapped entities. These geospatial datasets, when linked with ownership and transaction history, form the backbone of a digital land registry.

However, the technical sophistication of GIS alone does not guarantee a reduction in conflicts unless it is coupled with robust digital registries that encapsulate legal ownership, encumbrances, succession histories, and rights associated with each parcel. Digital land registries serve as centralized databases where data on land ownership, tenure types, transfers, leases, and cadastral information are compiled in secure, searchable, and accessible formats. The advantages of such registries are numerous and profound. They minimize reliance on physical documents susceptible to loss or alteration and provide institutions—government land agencies, courts, lawyers, community leaders—and the general public with real-time data that can verify claims and detect inconsistencies promptly. This transparency is pivotal in deterring fraudulent land sales, double revenue payments, and overlapping allocations. Moreover, a well-maintained digital registry reduces bureaucratic delays and corruption risks by automating processes such as property title verification, fee payments, and transaction registrations.

Beyond the technical measures, the implementation of digital land registries has a social justice component. Land ownership in Ghana is not only a matter of economic wealth but also identity, lineage, and community standing. Digital registries have the potential to democratize access to land information, allowing marginalized groups, including women, youth, and minority clans historically excluded from formal tenure processes, to assert and protect their rights more effectively. Mobile applications linked to these digital registries represent a critical user-friendly interface that makes land information accessible even to those in remote or underserved regions. Given the widespread adoption of mobile phones across Ghana, including the proliferation of smartphones and increasing internet penetration, mobile platforms allow users to search for titles, confirm ownership, apply for registrations, and even report disputes or irregularities through simple applications. This accessibility diminishes information asymmetry, empowers individuals, and fosters community-based monitoring of land ownership and use.

The potential for mobile applications to function as conflict-prevention tools extends beyond access to records. Interactive applications can facilitate the reporting and mediation of disputes before they escalate. For instance, users can submit geo-tagged evidence of contested boundaries or encroachments directly to local authorities or customary councils via mobile platforms. This real-time reporting mechanism supports proactive conflict resolution and aids in compiling dispute-related data that can inform policy and interventions. Furthermore, mobile apps can deliver educational content about land rights, processes for registration, and the importance of transparent land management. Such digital literacy initiatives are key in contexts where traditional practices and statutory laws sometimes clash, enabling citizens to navigate the legal landscape more effectively.

One cannot overlook the broader governance implications of digitizing land records. Centralization of land information in digital formats necessitates clear frameworks for data privacy, security, and interoperability among agencies. The success of digital land registries hinges on collaborative governance models that incorporate traditional authorities, government departments, civil society, and technology providers. In Ghana, the Land Use and Spatial Planning Authority (LUSPA), the Lands Commission, and the Ministry of Lands and Natural Resources have embarked on ambitious reforms to consolidate land information systems digitally, albeit with varying degrees of success due to institutional inertia, funding constraints, and capacity gaps. These efforts are frequently supported by international partners who bring technical expertise, equipment, and capacity building. However, technology must not inadvertently centralize power solely within formal state actors at the expense of customary custodians who play a vital role in land stewardship. The ideal digital registry system marries the rich local knowledge of customary landowners with the precision and accountability offered by technology, promoting legitimacy and broad acceptance.

The operationalization of digital land registries is not without challenges. Ghana's diverse land tenure systems—customary, freehold, leasehold, and statutory—require flexible digital frameworks that can accommodate varied ownership forms and rights. Digitizing the myriad of existing paper records and validating their accuracy demands extensive resources, expert personnel, and political will. Moreover, resistance may arise from actors who benefit from opaque systems, including fraudulent land dealers and corrupt officials. Overcoming such resistance calls for strong legal backing, transparency measures, and public engagement campaigns. Technical challenges include ensuring that GIS data and digital registries remain up to date, especially given rapid urban expansion and migration patterns that continuously redefine land uses. Adequate infrastructure, such as reliable internet connectivity, cloud storage, and cybersecurity protections, is imperative to safeguard the integrity of digital land data.

Despite these obstacles, the long-term benefits of digital land registries are compelling. They forge pathways toward reducing land conflicts by providing irrefutable, easily accessible proof of ownership and boundaries. This clarity diminishes ambiguity and dispute onset; it expedites conflict resolution procedures by equipping adjudicators with precise data; and it deters disputes altogether by creating an environment hostile to fraudulent practices. Additionally, detailed, digitized land data underpins sound policy-making and urban planning. Government planners can use geospatial and registry data to identify areas prone to conflict, monitor environmentally sensitive zones, and regulate land use to balance development and conservation. Investors and developers similarly benefit from the certainty and security digital registries create, fostering confidence that stimulates investment while respecting community interests.

Case studies within Ghana reveal the transformative potential of digital solutions. In the rapidly urbanizing Greater Accra region, pilot projects incorporating GIS-based digital registries have helped clarify the chaotic land tenure landscapes of informal settlements. Residents who previously endured tenure insecurity and harassment from land speculators now engage with digital platforms to register their holdings, gaining legal protections and enabling access to services such as utilities and loans. In the agriculturally rich Ashanti Region, traditional councils working with government agencies have utilized mobile applications to record and manage customary land allocations, significantly reducing disputes arising from unclear succession or boundary disagreements. These examples underscore how technology bridges traditional and formal governance systems, facilitating integrated land management.

Moreover, international experience offers valuable lessons. Countries with similar challenges have reaped substantial benefits from digital land registries. Rwanda's Land Tenure Regularization Program, for example, revolutionized land ownership certainty by combining GIS mapping with community-based enumeration, digitizing titles, and establishing accessible registries. The program reduced disputes, spurred rural investment, and enhanced women's land rights, illustrating how digital registries supported by participatory mechanisms can generate inclusive outcomes. In Ghana, adopting a similar approach—grounded in local participation yet leveraging advanced technology—offers a promising pathway for comprehensive land conflict reduction.

Technology is also enabling innovative approaches to continuous land monitoring and dispute detection. Emerging tools such as remote sensing satellites and drones complement GIS by providing up-to-date imagery that can show land use changes indicative of encroachments or illegal developments. When integrated with digital registries, such technologies create dynamic systems capable of alerting authorities and communities to potential conflicts at early stages before they escalate into violent confrontations or protracted legal battles. These real-time monitoring capabilities foster a culture of accountability and stewardship essential for sustainable land governance in Ghana.

Critically, the human dimension remains central to the success of digital land registries. Effective implementation requires capacity building for land officers, traditional leaders, and community members to navigate and manage digital tools competently. Training programs must be tailored to cultural contexts and literacy levels, ensuring inclusivity. Public education campaigns that communicate the benefits and procedures associated with digital registries build trust and encourage uptake, while addressing fears related to data misuse or loss of customary control. Policies must also safeguard against the marginalization of communities who lack access to digital technologies, ensuring hybrid approaches accommodate paper or verbal records where necessary until full digital integration is viable.

In conclusion, the adoption of digital land registries in Ghana represents a pivotal step toward mitigating land conflicts that have long hindered social harmony and economic progress. By harnessing the precision of GIS mapping, the accessibility of mobile technology, and the accountability of centralized digital records, Ghana can usher in a new era of land management marked by transparency, security, and inclusivity. While challenges abound—institutional, technical, and sociocultural—the commitment to bridging customary practices with formal statutory frameworks through technology offers a transformative vision. Digital land registries are not merely databases; they are instruments of justice and development capable of empowering communities, fostering investor confidence, and sustaining national stability. As Ghana moves forward, embracing these technologies with strategic planning, broad participation, and ethical governance will be key to unlocking their full potential as catalysts for peace and prosperity in the land sector.

15.2 Geographic Information Systems (GIS)

In the ever-evolving landscape of land management in Ghana, the emergence of Geographic Information Systems (GIS) has heralded a new era of precision, transparency, and efficiency, promising to revolutionize how land conflicts are addressed and ultimately mitigated. GIS, at its core, is a sophisticated technology that integrates hardware, software, and data for capturing, managing, analyzing, and displaying geographically referenced information. When deployed effectively, it empowers land administrators, policymakers, traditional authorities, and community members with accurate spatial data to inform decision-making processes that are critical in the prevention and resolution of disputes over land ownership and use. The utilization of GIS in Ghana's land sector does not merely represent a technological upgrade; it signifies a paradigm shift towards digital governance that aligns with global best practices in land administration and conflict resolution.

One of the most profound impacts of GIS in Ghana's land management system lies in its ability to create comprehensive digital registries that map the full extent of land parcels with remarkable detail. Traditionally, land records in Ghana have been fraught with ambiguities and fragmentation—resulting from the coexistence of customary and statutory land tenure systems that often operate in parallel yet with limited integration. This duality has caused jurisdictional overlaps and ownership disputes exacerbated by inadequate documentation and paper-based land registries vulnerable to loss, damage, or manipulation. GIS technology provides a platform to digitize and centralize land records by creating precise, geo-referenced cadastral maps linked to ownership information. This digital transformation ensures that every parcel of land can be uniquely identified and tracked, reducing the incidences of overlapping claims that frequently ignite conflicts. Thus, the technology fosters greater legal certainty and enhances the integrity of land titles.

Beyond the realm of cadastral mapping, GIS serves as a powerful analytical tool capable of integrating multiple layers of information about land use, environmental conditions, demographic pressures, infrastructure, and administrative boundaries. Such spatial analysis is invaluable for identifying hotspots of potential conflict, understanding the root causes of disputes, and designing evidence-based interventions. For example, rapid urbanization around Accra and Kumasi has led to intense competition for land between informal settlers, indigenous communities, and investors. By overlaying datasets on population growth, land use patterns, and infrastructure developments within a GIS framework, land managers can pinpoint areas with conflicting claims or excessive subdivision, signaling the need for targeted conflict prevention or negotiation efforts. Moreover, the visualization capabilities of GIS help stakeholders—from government officials to traditional leaders and community members—comprehend complex spatial relationships in a more intuitive manner, fostering informed dialogue and participatory decision-making.

The integration of mobile applications with GIS further extends the reach and accessibility of land management tools to the grassroots level, a crucial factor given the diverse and dispersed nature of Ghanaian communities. Mobile technology proliferation has been rapid, and harnessing this ubiquity allows for real-time data collection, reporting, and updates on land status. Community members, chiefs, and land officers equipped with GPS-enabled smartphones can submit geo-tagged information concerning boundary changes, land transactions, or encroachments directly into centralized databases. This decentralized data acquisition method not only enhances the reliability and timeliness of land records but also democratizes access to land information, reducing information asymmetry—a key driver of land conflicts. Furthermore, these mobile platforms can incorporate dispute reporting features that alert relevant authorities when conflicts emerge, facilitating prompt mediation or legal intervention before disputes escalate.

The potential of GIS and digital registries to reduce land conflicts, however, extends beyond the technical capabilities of mapping and data management. Their success hinges on the institutional frameworks, legal reforms, and collaborative governance arrangements that underpin land administration in Ghana. A significant challenge has been the limited interoperability between customary land tenure systems governed by chiefs and elders and formal statutory land institutions such as the Lands Commission and Land Title Registry, each maintaining separate records and procedures. GIS presents an opportunity to bridge this divide by serving as a common platform that harmonizes land information across these parallel systems, fostering mutual recognition and legal clarity. Initiatives that engage traditional authorities in the digitization process, training them to use GIS tools and integrating customary land rights into digital registries bolster legitimacy and community buy-in, crucial ingredients for sustainable conflict resolution.

Nevertheless, the deployment of GIS in land management is not without challenges. The initial costs of technology acquisition, data digitization, and capacity building can be substantial, especially in rural areas where infrastructure and technical expertise are limited. Moreover, data privacy and security concerns must be carefully managed to prevent misuse of land information, which could ironically exacerbate conflicts or create avenues for fraud. There is also the cultural dimension to consider—communities accustomed to oral histories of land ownership may initially resist the formalization and public exposure of traditional land rights in digital formats. Attention to these dynamics through inclusive stakeholder engagement, transparent communication, and gradual integration strategies enhances the acceptability of GIS interventions.

On the policy front, the Ghanaian government has recognized the transformative potential of GIS, embedding its use in national frameworks for land administration and natural resource management. For instance, the National Land Policy advocates for the enhancement of land information systems through technological means, emphasizing the integration of customary and formal land tenure data to ensure national coherence. The establishment of the Ghana Open Data Initiative and efforts to digitize land registries across multiple regions have provided an enabling environment for scaling GIS applications. Additionally, partnerships with development agencies and private sector actors have facilitated the transfer of technical know-how and resources, expanding the footprint of GIS-enabled land management initiatives.

Case studies from pilot programs underscore the tangible benefits of GIS in conflict reduction. In the Eastern Region, for example, GIS-assisted mapping of community lands facilitated the clarification of boundaries between competing villages, averting a long-standing dispute that threatened social cohesion. Similarly, in peri-urban areas of Greater Accra, mobile GIS applications used by land officers and traditional authorities enabled swift resolution of illegal encroachments, balancing the pressures of urban expansion with respect for established land rights. These examples illustrate how GIS technology fosters a more proactive approach to land governance—shifting from reactive dispute settlement to preventive management rooted in reliable, accessible information.

The future prospects for GIS in Ghana's land sector are promising, particularly with the rise of emerging technologies such as remote sensing, drones, and blockchain. Remote sensing complements GIS by providing up-to-date satellite imagery that can be used to monitor land use changes, detect unauthorized developments, and assess environmental impacts—information vital for conflict prevention and sustainable management. Drones, deployed for aerial surveys, facilitate rapid and cost-effective acquisition of precise topographic data even in inaccessible areas. Blockchain technology, when integrated with GIS-based land registries, offers possibilities for immutable and transparent recording of land transactions, significantly reducing fraud and enhancing trust among stakeholders.

In sum, Geographic Information Systems represent a cornerstone innovation for transforming land management in Ghana, addressing the endemic challenges of overlapping claims, documentation deficits, and institutional fragmentation that fuel land conflicts. By digitizing and spatially organizing land data, GIS enables a more transparent, inclusive, and data-driven approach to land governance, promoting legal certainty and social harmony. Realizing this potential, however, requires concerted efforts beyond technology deployment—strengthening legal frameworks, building institutional capacities, fostering stakeholder collaboration, and embracing cultural realities. As Ghana continues to urbanize and its population grows, the strategic adoption of GIS and allied digital tools will be crucial in ensuring that land remains a source of wealth and stability rather than division and strife. The integration of mapping technology thus not only empowers administrators and communities but also lays the foundation for a more peaceful and prosperous land governance landscape in Ghana's future.

15.3 Mobile and Online Platforms

In recent years, the infusion of digital technology into land management systems has introduced profound opportunities to transform the way land conflicts are reported, analyzed, and resolved across Ghana. Mobile and online platforms stand at the forefront of this technological revolution, offering tools that promise increased transparency, accessibility, and efficiency in a domain long riddled with complexity and opacity. The innovative integration of Geographic Information Systems (GIS), digital land registries, and dedicated mobile applications points toward an enhanced capacity to reduce disputes by clarifying ownership, streamlining communication between stakeholders, and facilitating real-time dispute reporting. These technologies not only modernize the often fragmented and inconsistent traditional practices but also empower local communities, government institutions, and legal practitioners in ways previously unimaginable. This exploration delves deeply into their current applications, latent potential, and the challenges they face within the unique socio-political and infrastructural landscape of Ghana.

One of the most transformative tools emerging in the realm of land conflict resolution is Geographic Information Systems (GIS). At its core, GIS integrates spatial and attribute data to create layered, interactive maps. In the Ghanaian context, this means that instead of relying solely on oral testimonies, paper-based maps, or outdated cadastral records, stakeholders can access detailed, up-to-date visualizations of land parcels. With GIS, boundaries are digitized and geographically pinpointed with precision using satellite imagery and ground surveys. This clarity of spatial information helps to preempt potential disputes by visibly delineating ownership and usage rights on an accessible platform. In the Greater Accra and Ashanti regions, pilot projects utilizing GIS have demonstrated promising results. For instance, local government authorities equipped with GIS-based cadastral systems have been able to detect overlapping claims early, intervening before conflicts escalate into violence. Moreover, GIS integrates environmental data, land use patterns, and demographic information, which assists planners and community leaders in making evidence-based decisions that account for sustainable development and equitable resource allocation.

Yet, the power of GIS transcends municipal planning; it redefines conflict resolution by shifting the focus from reactive litigation to proactive dispute avoidance. Through mobile-compatible GIS platforms, landholders and disputants increasingly have the means to access parcel information remotely, cross-check ownership details, and report discrepancies promptly. By digitizing boundary information, GIS also aids traditional leaders and dispute mediators, who historically relied heavily on subjective memory and local testimonies, by offering concrete, verifiable facts that soften contentious debates. Importantly, the inclusivity of GIS mapping also fuels community participation in land governance. Already marginalized groups, such as women and rural farmers, benefit from equitable representation when their parcels or claims are digitally recorded and geographically mapped, ensuring their stakes are acknowledged. However, the adoption of GIS is not without its hurdles. High initial investment costs, the need for technical expertise, and concerns about data privacy remain persistent barriers. Furthermore, the accuracy and reliability of GIS depend heavily on the quality of spatial data input, which in regions with poor infrastructure or historical record-keeping challenges can limit effectiveness. Thus, while GIS holds great promise for clarifying land tenure and reducing conflicts, its deployment requires sustained government commitment, capacity building, and community sensitization to reap full benefits.

Complementing GIS, digital land registries have emerged as a critical instrument in Ghana's efforts to modernize land administration and stem the tide of disputes. Traditionally, land records have been maintained in physical form, housed in regional land registries often plagued by inadequate storage, loss, forgery, and corruption. These weaknesses create fertile ground for conflicting claims, double allocations, and legal ambiguities. The establishment of digital registries, facilitated by policies such as the Land Administration Project (LAP) and the more recent digital transformation initiatives, seeks to address these challenges by creating centralized, secure, and verifiable repositories of land ownership data. By converting paper deeds into digital formats linked with biometric verification and secured through encryption, Ghana aims to make the registration process more transparent, user-friendly, and resistant to fraudulent manipulation.

The advantages of digital registries in land conflict prevention are multifold. Firstly, they reduce the probabilistic occurrence of overlapping titles by ensuring that every parcel of land has a unique identifier linked to its owner, geographic coordinates, and transaction history. This level of standardization minimizes errors created by inconsistent naming conventions, lost documents, and informal transfers. Secondly, digitization accelerates responsiveness; land stakeholders no longer need to traverse multiple offices over days or weeks to verify titles or lodge grievances, as many services can be accessed online or via integrated mobile platforms. This convenience increases the likelihood of prompt dispute resolution before conflicts escalate into violent confrontations. Thirdly, digital registries enhance accountability among government officers by embedding audit trails that reveal who accessed or amended a record and when, thereby discouraging corrupt practices which have historically undermined trust in land institutions.

Examples from the Eastern and Volta regions demonstrate the incremental successes of digital registries. Community elders and government officials report more efficient tracking of inheritance claims and fewer cases of land grabbing, as land titles linked securely in the system obviate the "guesswork" that previously dominated customary claims. Moreover, integrating digital registries with alternative dispute resolution mechanisms enables disputants to trigger mediation processes or appeal electronically, reducing the time and cost barriers traditionally facing land conflict resolution. Importantly, digital registries also integrate with taxation and land valuation systems, empowering governments to generate reliable revenue streams that fund further modernization efforts. Despite these benefits, challenges persist. Digital illiteracy, internet connectivity issues, and lack of trust in digital systems among older generations slow full adoption, particularly in rural communities. Additionally, programming the systems to accommodate complexities such as communal lands, customary tenures with multiple stakeholders, and customary land sales remains a nuanced technical and cultural challenge. Therefore, while digital registries are a cornerstone for future conflict reduction, their design and rollout must be context-sensitive, inclusive, and backed by extensive education campaigns to bridge the digital divide.

Alongside GIS and digital registries, mobile applications specifically designed for land management have emerged as powerful tools that put conflict reporting and resolution capabilities directly in the hands of ordinary citizens. Mobile phones, pervasive even in rural Ghana, offer an unparalleled platform for democratizing access to land-related information and services. Developers and government agencies have created applications that enable users to report land disputes in real time, upload images or videos as evidence, and receive guidance on the next procedural steps. Such apps also provide alerts about suspicious transactions, land sales, and court decisions, acting as early warning systems that enable communities and authorities to act swiftly.

For example, the LandRX mobile app, piloted in the Northern Region, allows farmers and communal landowners to register conflicts as incidents, tagging geolocations and pertinent details. This crowdsourced data flows into a centralized dashboard accessible to local magistrates, dispute mediators, and chiefs, ensuring that no dispute remains hidden or unregistered. By shortening communication channels, the app reduces delays and bottlenecks that often exacerbate frustrations and violence. In parallel, mobile applications like "Chieftaincy Land Connect" empower traditional leaders by offering a consolidated platform to record customary land transactions and resolutions, harmonizing oral traditions with digital records in a user-friendly interface. These apps promote transparency, reducing suspicions that leaders are circumventing justice or colluding to allocate land unfairly.

Mobile platforms also extend educational outreach by embedding legal information and guidelines on land rights, inheritance laws, and dispute mechanisms. This fosters a more informed citizenry that can recognize and resist exploitative schemes or unlawful encroachments. Furthermore, by interfacing with SMS-based alert systems, these platforms accommodate users with limited smartphone access, ensuring inclusivity. The interactive potential of mobile apps, coupled with social media integration, encourages community dialogue, consensus building, and dissemination of best practices for peaceful resolutions. However, the creation and sustainability of such applications face technical, financial, and linguistic barriers. Ghana's multilingual society demands apps to be culturally tailored and available in several local languages to ensure full accessibility. Moreover, inconsistent internet connectivity, cybersecurity threats, and the need for continuous technical support can hamper usage rates and data integrity. Thus, while mobile applications revolutionize dispute reporting, they must be embedded within broader capacity building and infrastructure development frameworks.

Critically, the synergy of GIS, digital registries, and mobile applications does not merely enhance individual tools but together crafts an integrated ecosystem for land conflict resolution. Linking GIS mapping layers with digital registries bridges spatial and legal documentation gaps, offering multi-dimensional verification of land tenure claims that strengthen case adjudication. When mobile apps feed real-time incident reports into this integrated system, decision-makers gain a comprehensive, dynamic overview of conflict hotspots, enabling targeted intervention. Ghana's Ministry of Lands and Natural Resources has recognized this potential, moving toward a unified platform that harmonizes data from diverse sources. Such integrated systems are critical given that land conflicts rarely arise from singular issues but from overlapping factors including undocumented customary rights, urban encroachment, inheritance ambiguities, and commercial pressure.

This integrated digital approach also reshapes the roles of traditional authorities and legal actors. Chiefs, traditionally the custodians of customary land, can supplement their knowledge and memory with interactive digital maps and registries, reducing disagreements rooted in misinterpretation. Legal practitioners benefit from rapid access to authenticated evidence, accelerating dispute resolution while lowering procedural costs. For government officials, these advancements improve land use planning, reduce administrative bottlenecks, and enhance national economic development prospects by building investor confidence through secure land tenure. On the citizen side, enhanced transparency and communication minimize tensions fueled by misinformation or exclusion from land governance processes.

Nonetheless, the implementation of such digital ecosystems necessitates vigilant attention to inclusivity and equity to avoid deepening pre-existing inequalities. Women, youth, and marginalized populations, who already face limited access to land and justice, may be excluded from benefiting from these technologies due to socioeconomic barriers or inadequate digital literacy. Thus, design principles must emphasize ease of use, localized language options, and community engagement initiatives to foster broad-based acceptance and adoption. Moreover, data protection and privacy safeguards are paramount to prevent misuse of sensitive land information, which could otherwise exacerbate tensions or facilitate corruption. Ensuring data sovereignty and clear protocols on who can access and amend records remains an ethical imperative alongside technological development.

In conclusion, mobile and online platforms manifest as critical instruments in Ghana's quest to modernize land administration and quell the cycles of land disputes that disrupt social harmony and economic progress. The strategic application of GIS mapping enhances clarity and evidence-based decision-making, digital land registries inject transparency and security into ownership records, and mobile applications democratize dispute reporting and legal education. Collectively, these technologies hold transformative promise when applied thoughtfully within Ghana's unique cultural and institutional frameworks. Their success depends not simply on technical deployment but on an inclusive, participatory approach that balances innovation with respect for customary norms and legal traditions. Through sustained government support, cross-sector collaboration, and community empowerment, the digital revolution in land governance can cultivate a future where land conflicts are minimized, access to justice is broadened, and the rich resource of Ghana's lands is managed sustainably for generations to come.

CHAPTER 16

A HOLISTIC FRAMEWORK FOR SUSTAINABLE LAND CONFLICT RESOLUTION

16.1 Integrating Customary and Statutory Systems

In the complex landscape of land governance in Ghana, the challenge of integrating customary and statutory systems stands as both a formidable obstacle and a vital opportunity. These dual frameworks, each rooted in distinct historical, cultural, and legal traditions, have long operated in parallel, occasionally intersecting with tensions that fuel conflicts and impede effective land administration. The customary system, deeply embedded in local traditions and community norms, governs the vast majority of land in Ghana, especially in rural areas. It is administered by chiefs and elders, embodying centuries-old practices that resonate with the social fabric of communities. On the other hand, the statutory system, deriving its authority from formal laws and government institutions, seeks to provide a standardized, legally enforceable framework for land rights and transactions, often tailored to meet the demands of modernization, urbanization, and economic development. The crux of integration lies in harmonizing these two systems so that they complement rather than contradict each other, forging a cohesive approach that respects local customs while ensuring clarity, security, and fairness under the law.

A central element of this integration process involves recognizing the strengths and limitations inherent in both customary and statutory systems. Customary land tenure is flexible, adaptive, and deeply participatory, closely linking land rights to lineage, community identity, and social responsibilities. However, it is also characterized by ambiguities in ownership, fragmented jurisdiction due to overlapping claims, and a lack of formal documentation that often complicates legal verification and enforcement. Conversely, the statutory system offers clarity, transparency, and formal mechanisms for land registration and dispute resolution, but it tends to be rigid, top-down, and alien to local practices, sometimes marginalizing traditional authorities and excluding vulnerable groups from meaningful participation. Therefore, any model for cooperation must seek a synergistic blend that institutionalizes traditional adjudicatory processes within the broader legal framework and establishes formal recognition of customary rights and authorities without compromising legal certainty.

Legal reform emerges as a pivotal strategy in this endeavor. One promising approach is the enactment of laws that explicitly acknowledge and incorporate customary land tenure systems within the national land policy. Ghana's Land Act, the Land Title Registration Law, and other related statutes have begun to pave the way for harmonization by legally recognizing the authority of traditional leaders in land administration, subject to defined statutory procedures. This creates a foundation for customary authorities to act as custodians of land and initial adjudicators of disputes, with statutory courts and regulatory bodies providing oversight, appeal mechanisms, and final enforcement. Yet, these reforms must go beyond mere legal recognition. They need to embed procedural safeguards that guarantee transparency, prevent abuses of power, and promote inclusiveness, ensuring that women, youth, and marginalized groups secure their rightful claims within customary domains. Without deliberate policy prescriptions and robust enforcement mechanisms, reforms risk being symbolic, leaving the underlying fissures unhealed.

Moreover, the formal incorporation of customary land practices within statutory frameworks requires innovative institutional arrangements. Hybrid institutions that blend traditional leadership with government land officials offer a practical model for cooperation. These bodies, composed of chiefs, elders, municipal authorities, and legal practitioners, can jointly oversee land allocation, registration, dispute resolution, and community sensitization. Such collaborations facilitate mutual trust building and knowledge exchange, empowering traditional authorities with legal literacy and statutory officers with cultural competence. By meeting regularly, these institutions ensure consistent application of agreed norms, mitigate jurisdictional conflicts, and respond more efficiently to emerging land issues. For instance, pilot projects in several Ghanaian districts have demonstrated success where land secretariats coordinate efforts between customary and statutory actors, resulting in more transparent land transactions and fewer conflicts. The challenge remains scaling these successes nationally, requiring political will, adequate funding, and capacity building tailored to local contexts.

Community engagement constitutes a third keystone in the integration model. Land conflicts often stem from disconnects between governance structures and the people they serve, particularly when customary systems are undermined or statutory processes are too technical and distant. Inclusive participation of community members, especially those vulnerable to exclusion, fosters legitimacy, ownership, and shared responsibility for land stewardship. Engagement can take many forms, such as participatory mapping exercises that document land boundaries according to both customary knowledge and formal surveys, public forums where rights holders discuss land issues collaboratively, and educational campaigns that explain legal rights and dispute procedures. These measures demystify land administration, reduce misinformation, and empower local populations to resolve conflicts amicably before they escalate. Furthermore, the integration process benefits from harnessing indigenous dispute resolution mechanisms embedded in customary governance—such as mediation, arbitration, and reconciliation—within the statutory framework, legitimizing these approaches through legal codification and administrative support. This culturally sensitive blend not only alleviates the courts' burden but also strengthens social cohesion, as disputes are settled in ways that resonate with community values.

Technology provides an indispensable catalyst for synthesizing traditional and formal systems into a more coherent whole. Digital land information management systems, geographic information technologies (GIS), and mobile applications are transforming land governance worldwide, and Ghana is poised to leverage these tools to bridge customary and statutory divides. One vital technological innovation is the development of integrated land registries that combine formal titles with customary claims, creating transparent, accessible databases that reflect the true complexity of land tenure on the ground. Such registries help prevent multiple allocations and fraudulent sales by providing a single authoritative source of land information, recorded with the involvement of customary custodians to ensure accuracy.

Additionally, technological platforms can facilitate dispute resolution by enabling remote mediation sessions, tracking case progress, and disseminating timely updates to stakeholders. Mobile technology also enhances community participation by allowing citizens to document land transactions, submit complaints, and receive notifications in real time, fostering greater accountability. The successful digitization of customary lands, however, requires careful design to respect confidentiality, address digital literacy gaps, and maintain traditional decision-making dynamics while improving transparency.

The synthesis of these elements—legal reform, institutional innovation, community participation, and technology—points toward comprehensive strategies that transcend binary oppositions between customary and statutory systems. Rather than viewing them as competing or hierarchical, integration models envision a pluralistic legal order where customary land rights are formally recognized and customary authorities operate within a regulated environment that ensures accountability and equity. This pluralism acknowledges the vitality of local customs in maintaining social order and land access while safeguarding individual security of tenure and facilitating economic development through formal land markets. Ghana's experience demonstrates that success depends heavily on context-specific adaptation, continuous dialogue among stakeholders, and political commitment to coordination across government ministries, traditional leadership councils, civil society organizations, and development partners.

A particularly instructive model is the collaborative framework developed in the Central Region, where structured dialogues between chiefs, government land officials, and community representatives have resulted in jointly created land use plans and conflict resolution protocols that respect both customary boundaries and statutory requirements. These frameworks, supported by training programs that build the capacities of customary leaders in legal and technical matters, strengthen the interface between governance levels. Furthermore, monitoring mechanisms involving community watchdog groups have emerged, overseen by these joint committees to report violations and mediate early conflict signals. Such embedded oversight functions help preserve the credibility of institutions, ensure compliance with regulations, and foster a culture of transparency that diminishes corruption and favoritism.

To advance integration, reforms must also address systemic challenges that undermine cooperation. Chief among these is the imbalance of power between customary authorities and formal institutions, which sometimes leads to contestations and parallel claims that deepen disputes. Efforts to harmonize land systems should include clear delineation of jurisdictional boundaries, with statutory bodies respecting the legitimacy and autonomy of customary rulers within agreed limits, while customary authorities recognize the supremacy of national laws on land policy and human rights standards. Capacity disparities also persist, as many traditional leaders lack formal legal training, while government officials may not appreciate the nuances of customary tenure. Targeted training and exchange programs, including secondments and joint workshops, can foster mutual understanding and technical competence. Moreover, addressing entrenched corruption and politicization within land administration requires strengthening accountability frameworks, backed by community monitoring and independent oversight bodies.

Another thorny issue is the integration of gender-sensitive approaches in both systems. Customary land tenure often marginalizes women's land rights, relying on patriarchal lineage and inheritance practices that exclude or undervalue female claims. Statutory laws generally provide more explicit protections for women, but enforcement gaps persist. Therefore, integrated models must include deliberate mechanisms to protect and enhance women's land tenure security, combining community education, the reform of customary norms, and legal empowerment initiatives. Women's participation must be ensured at all levels of land governance, from decision-making in family and community land management to representation within hybrid institutions and access to formal dispute resolution channels. Without addressing gender dynamics, integration efforts risk perpetuating inequalities that contribute to social instability.

In terms of practical steps, policymakers might consider establishing multi-tiered land governance frameworks that formalize cooperation at local, district, and national levels. At the community level, customary authorities could manage land allocation and dispute mediation with formal recording into district land registries. At the district level, hybrid land management boards with representatives from traditional leadership, local government, and civil society could oversee land use planning, registration verification, and conflict monitoring. Nationally, coordination bodies within the Ministry of Lands and Natural Resources could harmonize policies, support capacity building, and oversee technology deployment to ensure standardization and interoperability of data systems. This vertical integration fosters a continuum of responsibility, reinforces checks and balances, and creates streamlined channels for dispute escalation and resolution.

The international experience also offers valuable lessons. Countries like Botswana and Namibia have implemented land governance systems that respect customary tenure while accommodating statutory frameworks, relying heavily on decentralization, community-based adjudication, and digital integration. Ghana can adapt best practices by focusing on endogenous solutions informed by local values and conditions. Donor agencies and development partners have roles to support pilot initiatives, fund research, and provide technical assistance, while recognizing that ultimate sustainability depends on domestic ownership and political commitment.

Sustainability of integrated land governance further requires ongoing research and feedback mechanisms. Establishing data collection and analysis units that monitor the incidence of land conflicts, track resolution effectiveness, and collect community perceptions can provide empirical evidence to refine policies incrementally. This evidence-based approach enables adaptive management that responds to emerging challenges such as climate change pressures, urban sprawl, and demographic shifts. Inclusion of academic institutions and civil society in these processes deepens participatory governance and knowledge generation.

Ultimately, the integration of customary and statutory systems in Ghana's land governance is not merely a technical exercise but a transformative socio-political project. It demands reimagining the relationship between tradition and modernity in land administration, acknowledging that neither system alone can meet the evolving demands of Ghana's society.

Through patient dialogue, respect for cultural diversity, legal innovation, and technological advancement, it is possible to build an integrated land governance framework that stabilizes disputes, enhances tenure security, empowers communities, and stimulates sustainable development. Such a framework can serve as a beacon for other African nations grappling with similar dualities, demonstrating that harmonious coexistence of customary and statutory land governance is achievable and beneficial for national cohesion and prosperity. The journey toward this integration is ongoing, requiring perseverance, inclusiveness, and a shared vision that places people and equitable access to land at its core.

16.2 Policy and Institutional Coordination

Effective governance and seamless collaboration lie at the heart of transforming land conflict resolution in Ghana into a system that is both just and sustainable. The intricate web of land disputes, shaped by historical, cultural, socio-economic, and legal complexities, demands a governance architecture that not only harmonizes the clashing interests but also integrates the traditional and formal frameworks that have coexisted, often uneasily, over centuries. To establish an environment whereby land conflicts can be addressed proactively, it is imperative to conceive strategies that promote policy coherence, institutional synergy, and community inclusivity, all the while anchoring these developments in robust technological advancements. This multi-dimensional approach entails a careful recalibration of legal reforms, deliberate strengthening of institutional linkages, empowered traditional structures, engaged citizenry, and the creative deployment of technology as a facilitator rather than a disruptor in the domain of land governance.

Legal reform must be considered the cornerstone upon which the edifice of coordinated governance rests. Ghana's dual land tenure system poses a unique challenge because it requires a delicate balancing act between statutory legislation and customary land rights. Historically, legal frameworks have often leaned disproportionately either towards formal statutory processes or veered excessively towards traditional methods without harmonizing the two. This imbalance has resulted in overlapping jurisdictions, conflicting authority claims, and procedural inefficiencies that have exacerbated land conflicts rather than resolving them. Therefore, policy efforts should prioritize the comprehensive revision and updating of laws governing land ownership, registration, transfer, and dispute resolution, ensuring they recognize and validate customary tenure systems within the wider legal structure. Doing so would not only impart a legitimate voice to traditional authorities but also minimize legal ambiguity where customary practices diverge from statutory norms. The revised legal framework should also introduce clearer guidelines on land rights documentation that are accessible and understandable to all stakeholders, thereby reducing incidences of unclear or fraudulent land titling which act as ignition points for disputes. In this context, strengthening land administration laws to promote transparency, accountability, and efficiency could further reduce procedural bottlenecks, curtail corruption, and foster trust among land users.

Beyond legal reform, the challenge of institutional coordination demands a strategic overhaul of how various agencies, authorities, and stakeholders converge and communicate in land matters. Currently, fragmented responsibilities and weak inter-agency collaboration undermine resolution efforts, often resulting in duplicated efforts or contradictory decisions. An effective strategy to rectify this begins with the establishment of an integrated institutional platform or a central coordination mechanism that links traditional councils, land management authorities, judiciary bodies, local government units, and sector ministries such as those responsible for agriculture, urban development, and environment. Such a platform should facilitate continuous information sharing, joint decision-making, and synchronized policy implementation. It must also define clear roles and responsibilities while creating accountability pathways to monitor performance and compliance. Regular convenings of multi-stakeholder forums where government officials, traditional leaders, community representatives, and legal practitioners can interact would promote mutual understanding and collaborative problem-solving. The presence of these dialogues breaks down silos and nurtures trust that is vital for harmonized actions on sensitive land issues.

Crucially, any attempt to coordinate institutions must not sideline the powerful and often underappreciated role traditional authorities play in land governance. Chiefs, elders, and customary land custodians wield considerable influence because their legitimacy is embedded in the cultural fabric of communities. Engaging traditional systems as partners rather than relics of the past can anchor dispute resolution in local values and practices, enabling more socially acceptable outcomes. Strategies to this effect include formalizing the roles of traditional leaders within the land governance architecture by granting them defined responsibilities in mediation and land registration processes under statutory supervision. Capacity building and training programs tailored specifically for these traditional custodians can enhance their understanding of modern legal concepts and administrative procedures, empowering them to navigate the dual systems more effectively. Moreover, the formal recognition of alternative dispute resolution processes, often led by traditional authorities, within the wider judiciary framework can provide pragmatic and expedient pathways to settle disputes. Institutional coordination efforts should also strive to prevent power abuses and ensure that traditional systems operate within principles of fairness, inclusivity, and respect for human rights, thereby making the customary route a viable complement to statutory mechanisms.

Engagement with communities, especially those most vulnerable to land conflicts, constitutes another pivotal pillar in fostering effective governance. Inclusive participation ensures policies and dispute resolution initiatives are responsive to the lived realities of land users, thereby enhancing their legitimacy and acceptance. Community engagement should transcend token representation and instead aim for genuine involvement in decision-making, monitoring, and feedback processes. Educational outreach programs that demystify land laws, property rights, and conflict resolution procedures can empower citizens to assert their rights knowledgeably and to seek appropriate channels for redress. Similarly, creating platforms for dialogue within communities fosters collective problem-solving and reduces suspicions that often fuel tensions. Institutional mechanisms should promote gender-sensitive approaches recognizing the marginalized status of women and youth in access to land and participation in governance. By incorporating diverse voices, policy and institutional frameworks will be more reflective of societal dynamics and adaptable to evolving challenges.

Another transformative dimension lies in harnessing technology to unify, streamline, and enhance land governance and dispute resolution. Ghana's experience with land registration and records management has often been hampered by fragmented data systems, poor accessibility, and vulnerabilities to manipulation. Digitalization offers an avenue to address these weaknesses by enabling the creation of comprehensive, centralized, and easily retrievable land information databases. Integrating geographic information systems (GIS) and satellite imaging can bring unprecedented clarity to land boundaries, ownership histories, and usage patterns, thus reducing ambiguities that provoke conflicts. Mobile technology and online platforms can facilitate easier public access to land records, complaint lodging, and status tracking, making governance more transparent and responsive. Moreover, technology can support arbitration and mediation by providing virtual meeting forums, documentation archives, and expert advisory services, bridging geographical and socio-cultural divides. However, deploying technology requires careful consideration of the digital divide and data privacy concerns to ensure that access is equitable and information is protected from misuse. Capacity building among land officers, traditional leaders, and the public on digital literacy is essential to maximizing the benefits of these innovations.

To synthesize these elements into coherent strategies, the adoption of a multi-sectoral and multi-level governance model becomes imperative. This model envisages a framework where national policies align seamlessly with regional and local actions, engaging a constellation of actors who complement each other's mandates while avoiding jurisdictional conflicts. At the core, an overarching national land policy should articulate clear principles for equity, efficiency, and environmental sustainability, serving as a compass for institutional behavior. This policy must explicitly advocate for the integration of customary tenure systems and endorse inclusive approaches that recognize the rights of marginalized groups. It should also prescribe frameworks for legal reform, institutional coordination, and technological deployment, enshrining accountability and conflict prevention as central tenets. To operationalize this policy, government ministries and agencies must collaborate through designated inter-ministerial committees that oversee implementation, monitor performance, and adjust strategies based on iterative learning. These committees would be tasked with mediating between competing priorities such as economic development, environmental protection, and social justice, ensuring balanced outcomes.

At the regional and district levels, traditional authorities, land secretariats, and local assemblies form the frontline of governance, where policy translates into practice. Empowering these entities through adequate resources, clear mandates, and training transforms them into effective custodians capable of proactive conflict mitigation and responsive dispute handling. Building their capacity to collect, manage, and share data transparently supports evidence-based decision-making. The involvement of civil society organizations at this level acts as a watchdog, participation facilitator, and advocate for vulnerable groups, injecting accountability and social equity into governance processes.

The success of policy and institutional coordination also hinges on fostering a culture of collaboration characterized by trust, dialogue, and shared goals. This cultural dimension requires sustained efforts to overcome historic rivalries, mistrust between formal and traditional authorities, and skepticism among communities towards government institutions. Trust-building measures might include joint training workshops, shared community projects, transparency in resource allocation, and mutual grievance mechanisms that allow grievances to be aired constructively before escalating into conflicts. Effective communication channels that keep all stakeholders informed and engaged create a sense of ownership and collective responsibility for land governance outcomes.

Moreover, policy frameworks must not remain static but evolve responsively to emerging challenges such as rapid urbanization, climate change, and evolving socio-economic dynamics that influence land use and tenure. Regular policy reviews anchored in data and stakeholder consultations enable adaptation and innovation in governance approaches. For instance, emerging land issues like speculative land grabs, environmental degradation, and resettlement conflicts demand new regulatory tools and institutional competencies that traditional laws may not fully encompass. Coordination strategies should thus institutionalize mechanisms for continuous learning, research, and knowledge exchange among actors involved in land governance.

An often overlooked but essential ingredient in effective coordination lies in securing sustainable financing for land governance initiatives. Governments, often constrained by limited budgets, must explore innovative financing mechanisms including public-private partnerships, donor collaborations, and community-based contributions to underwrite reforms and institutional strengthening programs. Transparent budget management tied to performance indicators incentivizes efficient use of resources and engenders confidence among funders and beneficiaries alike.

In summary, the quest for effective governance and collaboration in Ghana's land conflict resolution must weave together progressive legal reforms that acknowledge the legitimacy of customary systems within the rule of law; robust institutional linkages that ensure coordinated action across government layers and traditional authorities; deep community engagement that empowers citizens and elevates marginalized voices; and judicious application of technology to reinforce transparency and efficiency. These elements must be underpinned by a culture of cooperation, trust, and continuous learning, supported by sustainable financing and adaptive policy frameworks. Only through an integrated, holistic approach that respects the mosaic of Ghana's land tenure realities can a resilient, fair, and dynamic land governance regime emerge—one that mitigates conflicts, promotes equitable land distribution, fosters economic growth, and nurtures social cohesion for generations to come.

Future Directions and Innovations

As Ghana looks toward the future, the resolution of land conflicts demands more than mere continuation of past efforts; it requires a transformative reimagining grounded in emerging trends and innovative approaches that holistically address the complexities of land governance. The landscape of land conflict resolution in Ghana is dynamically evolving, shaped by rapid technological advancements, the interplay between customary and formal legal systems, increasing awareness and activism among communities, and shifting socio-political parameters. Consequently, the future calls for an integrated strategy that marries legal reforms, purposeful incorporation of traditional institutions, proactive community participation, and the power of technology to craft a sustainable and peaceful land administration regime.

At the forefront lies the imperative for comprehensive legal reform, aimed at harmonizing Ghana's dualistic land tenure framework. The current disparity between statutory laws and customary practices remains a profound source of confusion and contestation. Future legal reforms must strive for greater clarity and consistency, not by eroding customary land rights but by formally recognizing and embedding the roles traditional authorities play within the statutory framework. This calls for an adaptive legal architecture that accommodates flexibility while establishing clear procedural safeguards. Efforts must focus on streamlining land registration processes, protecting legitimate occupancy rights, and simplifying dispute resolution to reduce bottlenecks and inhibit exploitation by powerful interests. Crucially, reform processes ought to be inclusive, engaging traditional leaders, legal practitioners, community stakeholders, and policymakers jointly to ensure that solutions reflect the lived realities of diverse Ghanaian communities rather than a top-down imposition of laws.

Equally essential to future progress is the revitalization and meaningful empowerment of traditional dispute resolution mechanisms. Chiefs and elders have long been custodians of community cohesion and land stewardship, employing culturally rooted norms and consensus-building techniques that command respect among local populations. Rather than viewing customary systems as archaic or as obstacles to modernization, the future must recognize them as vital complementary pillars alongside the formal judiciary. This involves capacity building for traditional authorities, including training on human rights adherence, gender sensitivity, and formal mediation techniques, to foster transparent and equitable outcomes. Moreover, mechanisms should be designed to formally integrate customary dispute resolution outcomes into the broader land governance framework, ensuring enforceability and reducing recourse to protracted litigation. Such integration, if handled with care and respect for tradition, promises to reduce conflict escalation, increase accessibility to justice—particularly for vulnerable groups—and preserve indigenous wisdom as a guiding compass for land matters.

Community engagement stands as the third transformative pillar in envisaging the future of land conflict resolution in Ghana. Sustainable change cannot be realized without the active participation and empowerment of affected communities, for they are often the primary victims and agents in land disputes. Moving beyond token consultations, future strategies must promote ongoing, meaningful dialogues that enable communities to articulate their interests, contribute to policy design, and monitor implementation of land governance frameworks. This community-led approach not only fosters ownership and trust but enhances social cohesion by building empathy and collective problem-solving capacity. Special efforts should be dedicated to including women, youth, minority groups, and marginalized populations, who frequently suffer disproportionate impacts from land conflicts yet remain underrepresented in decision-making arenas. Robust public education campaigns, awareness programs, and capacity-building workshops are indispensable tools for equipping citizens with knowledge of their rights and responsibilities, promoting peaceful dispute resolution, and counteracting misinformation which often fuels tensions.

Revolutionizing land administration through technology presents perhaps the most exhilarating frontier of future innovation. Ghana's land sector stands at the cusp of a digital transformation that holds unprecedented potential to enhance transparency, efficiency, and accessibility in land registration and conflict monitoring. Cutting-edge tools like geospatial mapping, blockchain-enabled land registries, and mobile platforms for conflict reporting can revolutionize how land rights are documented, verified, and enforced. For example, integrating satellite imagery with community-validated data allows accurate demarcation of customary boundaries, which are often ambiguous and a common source of conflicts. Blockchain technology offers possibilities for tamper-proof land title records, reducing fraud, corruption, and multiple sales. Meanwhile, mobile applications can facilitate real-time reporting of disputes or illicit land transactions, enabling timely interventions. However, the success of digital innovations depends crucially on bridging the digital divide; efforts must be made to ensure technological solutions are user-friendly, affordable, and inclusive of rural and underserved populations.

In parallel with technological adoption, the emergence of data-driven governance can immensely improve land conflict prevention and resolution. The accumulation and analysis of comprehensive land conflict data—disaggregated by region, type of dispute, parties involved, and resolution outcomes—can inform targeted interventions and policy adjustments. Employing artificial intelligence and predictive analytics, government agencies and traditional councils can anticipate hotspots of potential conflicts and allocate resources proactively. Institutionalizing independent land observatories or monitoring bodies that collate and publish accessible data will enhance accountability and promote informed public discourse. Further, evidence-based research linking land conflict patterns with broader socio-economic indicators such as migration, urbanization, and climate change can help formulate long-term strategic plans that address structural drivers rather than symptoms of land instability.

Another emerging trend poised to impact the future trajectory of land governance in Ghana is the growing role of multi-stakeholder collaboration and partnerships. The intricate nature of land conflicts, involving competing economic interests, political actors, and community groups, necessitates collective action that transcends institutional silos. Future directions must emphasize platforms for continuous dialogue among government institutions, traditional authorities, civil society organizations, legal professionals, investors, and academia. Such collaborative frameworks can facilitate knowledge sharing, conflict mediation, and coordinated policy implementation. International partnerships and exchange programs can also expose Ghanaian stakeholders to best practices and innovations from other jurisdictions facing similar challenges, fostering adaptive learning and context-sensitive application. By mobilizing diverse capacities, the sector can generate contextually grounded solutions that respect cultural heritage while embracing modern governance principles.

Climate change and environmental pressures introduce additional dimensions that the future of land conflict resolution cannot ignore. Expanding populations and unpredictable weather patterns intensify competition for fertile land and water resources, often igniting new conflicts or aggravating dormant ones. Future strategies must therefore incorporate sustainable land management principles that balance environmental conservation with economic use. This includes promoting agroforestry, soil restoration, and controlled urban expansion practices that mitigate degradation and reduce the scarcity that feeds disputes. Environmental impact assessments linked with land transactions and development projects should become standard practice, involving community consent as a non-negotiable component. In this context, conflict resolution mechanisms must be equipped to mediate not just ownership claims, but also disputes arising from environmental resource use, thus adapting to the evolving nature of land-related tensions.

Education and capacity building at all levels emerge as indispensable long-term investments for future resilience. Institutionalizing curricula on land governance and conflict resolution in schools, universities, and training institutes fosters a new generation of informed citizens and professionals equipped with the skills to navigate the complex interplay between traditional and statutory systems. Specialized training for judges, lawyers, and mediators on the nuances of Ghana's land tenure realities enhances the judiciary's capacity for fair and expedited adjudication. Likewise, capacitating traditional leaders with knowledge on human rights, property law, and conflict management builds trust and bridges the divide between customary and formal mechanisms. Community education campaigns that leverage local languages, cultural idioms, and media can demystify land laws and reduce misunderstandings. Thus, sustained investment in human capital development underpins the entire architecture of peaceful, equitable land governance.

The future also beckons a recalibration of power relations embedded in land governance. Historically, land conflicts in Ghana have often been aggravated by asymmetrical power dynamics—whether between investors and communities, chiefs and sub-chiefs, or government agencies and marginalized groups. To foster sustainable peace, future reforms must consciously foster equity by protecting the rights of vulnerable actors and limiting undue influence by powerful elites. This involves transparent, participatory decision-making processes where affected populations possess real agency. Institutions handling land must be held accountable through regular audits, grievance redress mechanisms, and citizen oversight committees. Empowering women, who under customary norms frequently face exclusion from land ownership despite being primary agricultural producers, is especially critical for justice and economic development. Gender-responsive policies and affirmative legal provisions can help redress historical imbalances and promote inclusive growth. Ultimately, the path forward relies on transforming land governance into an arena characterized by fairness, transparency, and shared benefit.

Reflecting on financial mechanisms, innovative funding models may catalyze more effective land conflict resolution and sustainable management in the future. Investments in land administration infrastructure and capacity are often constrained by budgetary limitations, which stymie necessary reforms. Exploring public-private partnerships, donor collaborations, and impact investment focused on land sector improvement could provide fresh resources and expertise. Additionally, governments might consider incentivizing community-led projects that promote conflict resolution and sustainable land use through grants or subsidies. Establishing dedicated land conflict resolution funds to support mediation, legal aid, and community dialogues ensures accessibility to justice for disenfranchised parties. Furthermore, integrating land tenure security into broader national development frameworks may unlock multi-sectoral funding streams, reinforcing the interdependence between secure land rights, poverty alleviation, and socio-economic stability.

Increasingly, gender and youth perspectives must inform the future of land conflict resolution. Ghana's youth represent a burgeoning demographic whose aspirations for land access, economic opportunity, and cultural continuity remain largely unmet, occasionally exacerbating tensions. Future strategies should actively incorporate youth voices in policy formulation and conflict resolution forums, recognizing their roles not only as potential conflict actors but as dynamic change agents. Technical and vocational training that links land rights with entrepreneurship can empower young people to contribute positively to sustainable land use and wealth creation. In parallel, addressing persistent gender disparities by advancing women's land ownership rights and dismantling discriminatory practices must remain priorities. Gender-sensitive conflict analysis and resolution modalities ensure that interventions protect rights and remedy specific vulnerabilities. Concretely, these inclusive approaches foster social cohesion and intergenerational equity, vital for long-term peace.

Legal pluralism, while posing challenges, can be harnessed creatively as a future strength. Rather than aiming solely to eradicate overlapping authority between statutory and customary systems, policies could conceptualize pluralism as an opportunity for adaptive governance that reflects Ghana's socio-cultural diversity. Innovative hybrid models might be institutionalized where traditional norms guide everyday resource management and minor disputes, while statute law intervenes in more complex or rights-sensitive cases. Formal mechanisms for dialogue and cooperation between courts and customary institutions could reduce contradictions and jurisdictional conflicts. Documentation and codification of customary laws—done collaboratively with traditional leaders and community members—could clarify norms and standards. Such hybridization, with clear roles and mutual respect, promises to preserve cultural legitimacy while ensuring legal certainty.

Cross-sectoral integration is increasingly necessary, recognizing that land conflicts intersect with broader issues such as urban planning, natural resource management, and economic development. Future land governance frameworks must therefore be embedded within multi-sectoral strategies that coordinate actions across ministries, agencies, and stakeholders. For instance, integrating land use planning with infrastructure development and environmental conservation prevents contradictory policies that create fertile grounds for disputes. Adopting a landscape approach that balances agricultural productivity, urban expansion, and ecosystem protection aligns economic gains with sustainability. Establishing inter-ministerial committees and joint monitoring units can enhance policy coherence and reduce fragmentation. This systemic perspective ensures that land governance contributes effectively to Ghana's national vision of inclusive growth and resilience.

To further aid peaceful land management in the future, harnessing the media and communication platforms is essential. Mass media, social media, and indigenous communication channels play a crucial role in shaping public perceptions, disseminating information, and mobilizing communities. Strategic use of media campaigns can foster awareness about lawful land use practices, dispute resolution avenues, and property rights. They can also counter misinformation and inflammatory narratives that often escalate tensions. Engaging influential community figures, opinion leaders, and youth advocates as ambassadors for peaceful land governance amplifies outreach and credibility. Exploring innovative formats such as community radio dramas, educational videos, and interactive social media forums creates spaces for dialogue and learning. Thoughtfully leveraging communication tools transforms them into engines for transparency, education, and trust-building.

Anticipating future challenges requires proactive contingency planning to build resilience within land governance systems. Conflicts are often triggered or worsened by sudden shocks, whether political upheavals, economic downturns, or natural disasters. Instituting early warning mechanisms that detect signs of emerging disputes and mobilize rapid response teams can mitigate escalation. This calls for strengthened institutional capacity in data collection, analysis, and coordinated action among land agencies, traditional authorities, and security forces. Developing emergency protocols, including mediation hotlines and community peace committees, creates ready-made channels for peaceful resolution. Moreover, embedding conflict sensitivity in all land-related policies and programs ensures that potential risks are carefully assessed and addressed prior to implementation. Such forward-looking preparedness builds durable institutions capable of withstanding and adapting to uncertainties.

The notion of sustainability itself must evolve to foreground social justice and intergenerational equity as core components in future land governance aspirations. Secure land tenure, peaceful dispute resolution, and equitable access to land resources are linchpins not only for immediate economic prosperity but for the broader idea of human dignity and empowerment. Future directions encourage viewing landlands not merely as economic commodities but as integral facets of social identity, heritage, and communal well-being. This paradigm shift advocates an ethos of shared stewardship where land users engage collaboratively in conserving landscapes and nurturing community resilience. Fostering inclusive governance, transparent decision-making, and respect for customary values simultaneously preserves cultural richness and promotes innovation. In this way, Ghana can chart a course that reconciles tradition with modernity, growth with equity, specificity with universality—crafting a land governance model that serves this generation and those to come.

In conclusion, the future of land conflict resolution in Ghana beckons an ambitious yet pragmatic pathway blending tradition, law, community, technology, and innovation. By embracing legal harmonization, empowering customary authorities, deepening community engagement, and harnessing digital tools, Ghana can transcend persistent land challenges that have long impeded social cohesion and development. This multidimensional approach, fortified by robust data systems, multi-stakeholder collaboration, environmental consciousness, education, and equitable governance, charts a roadmap for durable peace and prosperity rooted in land security. As the nexus of identity, livelihood, and power, land will continue to shape Ghana's trajectory—and the innovations and strategies embraced today will indelibly influence the nation's harmony, justice, and flourishing decades from now. The commitment to a future that integrates the wisdom of the past with the possibilities of the present heralds a new dawn for conflict resolution over lands in Ghana.

BIBLIOGRAPHY

Anon (2010), "2010 Population and Housing Census", www.Statsghana.gov.gh/popstats.html/. Accessed: 24 March 2015.

Anyidoho, N A; Amanquah, S T; and Clottey, E A (2008), "Chieftaincy Institutions and Land Tenure Security: Challenges, Responses and the Potential for Reform", *Technical Publication* No 77, Institute of Statistical, Social & Economic Research (ISSER), University of Ghana, Legon.

Asiama, S O (2002), "Comparative Study of Land Administration Systems", case study.

Brobbey, S A (2015), "Changing Face of the Law", Review of Ghana Law, vol. XXIII, p. 248.

Cittie, R (2006), "Land Title Registration; the Ghanaian Experience", Shaping the Change XXIII FIG Congress, Munich, Germany, pp 4–10.

Consultations for a World Bank Policy Research Report, pp. 106–150.

Ghana." *Report prepared for the World Bank*, (Land Institutions and Land Policy

Gladys Mensah v Stephen Mensah [2012] 1 SCGLR 391.

Iqbal, N and Gill, Z A (2000). The Concept of Land Ownership in Islam and Poverty Alleviation in Pakistan [with Comments]. The Pakistan Development Review, pp. 649–662.

Joint Committee of the American Congress on Surveying and Mapping and the American Society of Civil Engineers, Definitions of Surveying and Associated Terms 1978 (Rev). Reprinted 1989.

Kasanga, R K (1988), "Land Tenure and the Development Dialogue: The Myth Concerning Communal Landholding in Ghana", *Granta Editions Ltd*, Cambridge. pp. 12–25.

Kotey, E N A (2002), "Compulsory Acquisition of Land in Ghana:" *Does the 1992 Constitution Open New Vistas?*" in Toulmin, C; Lavigne Delville, P; and Traore, S (eds), The Dynamics of Resource Tenure in West Africa, IIED, London.

Kuntu-Mensah, P (2006), "On the Implementation of Land Title Registration in Ghana Promoting Land Administration and Good Governance" 5th FIG *Regional Conference*, Accra, Ghana, 8–11 March 2006.

Mahama, C and Dixon, M (2006), "Acquisition and affordability of land for housing in urban Ghana: a study in the formal land market dynamics". RICS Research paper series 6(10)

Ollenu, N A (1962), "Principles of Customary Land Law in Ghana". Sweet & Maxwell, London, p. 272.

Paaga, T D (2013), "Customary Land Tenure and Its Implications for Land Disputes in Ghana: Cases from Wa, Wechau And Lambussie", Department of African and General Studies University for Development Studies *International Journal of Humanities and Social Science* vol. 3, no. 18; October 2013.

Quartey v Martey [1959] GLR 377.

Salasai, S (1998), The concept of landownership: Islamic perspective. Bulletin Geoinformasi, 2(2), 285-304.

The Constitution of the Republic of Ghana (1992).

The 1,036th act of the parliament of the Republic of Ghana entitled Lands Act 2020. Retrieved from https://landwise-production.s3.amazonaws.com/2022/06/LAND-ACT-2020-ACT-1036.pdf.

The Lands Act (2020), extract from the Ghana Lands Act 2020 (ACT 1036).

Brown, William P, LS (MN), Communicator, July 2004 - (Publication of AELSLAGID).

Yongfang, Y and Liangi, Z (2013), "Theories and Diagnostic Methods of Land Use Conflicts". *Asian Agricultural Research 2013*, 5(4):, 70. Kaifeng, pp. 63–67.

Note:

"swt" - is the Arabic abbreviation meaning "May he (Allah) be glorified and exalted".

Ushr - tax (10%) paid on total agricultural output

PRODUCTION SPONSOR

Our Vision, Mission & Core Values

Vision

To render a first class professional service in land administration and management at competitive prices, thereby promoting a long term relationship with all client

Mission

To provide value-added surveying, Construction and engineering services for clients through innovation, foresight, integrity, aggressive performance, and service with character and purpose that brings honour to God

Core Values

Professionalism, Openness, fairness, innovation, teamwork and safety

ACCOMPLISHMENTS — AWARDS

- **IPMATIIC AFRICA AWARD (2014)**
  Quality service and Guarantee performance (2014)

- **GREEN RELIEF & COMMUNITY DEVELOPMENT - FOUNDATION AWARD**
  Legacies of excellence in service & Leadership

- **OSABARIMBA ROYAL AWARDS**
  Most innovative Business in Cape Coast (2022)

- **GHANA CHAMBER OF COMMERCE AWARDS**
  Company of the year (2018)

- **EUROPEAN BUSINESS ASSEMBLY**
  European quality award

CURRENT STATUS & SERVICES

- Well established land management consultancy managing over 25 customary (family and stool) Lands with a total land size of over 45,000 acres

- Sell litigation free lands for all kinds of projects

- Skills, knowledge & professionalism of land use related discipline

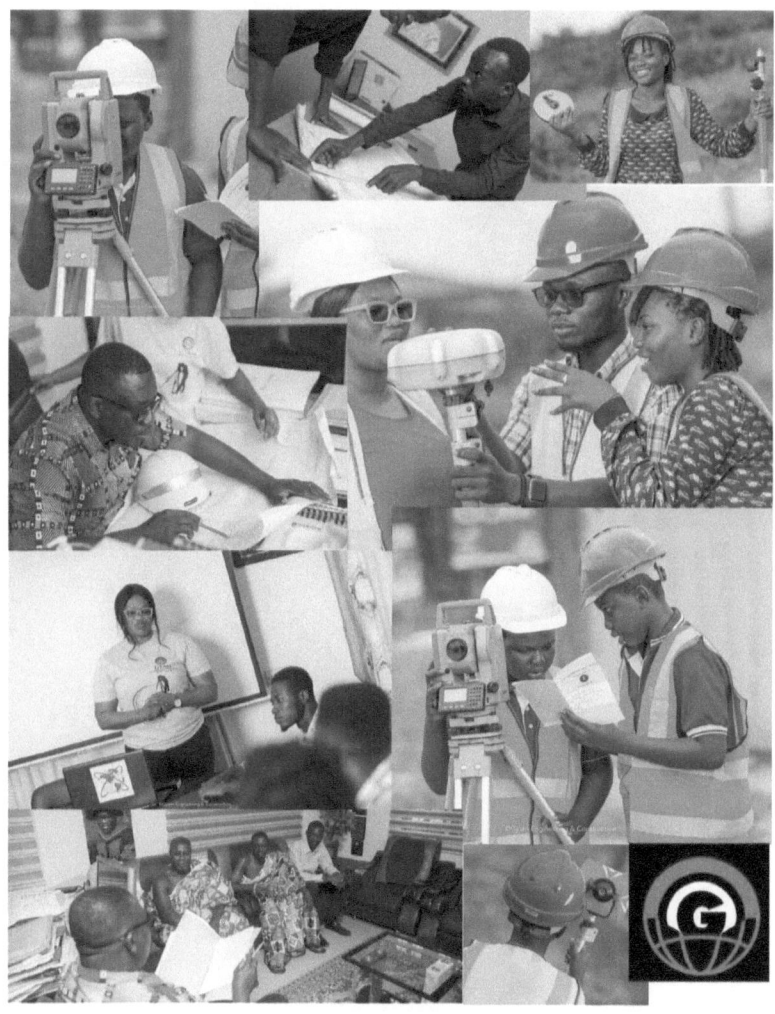

www.ingramcontent.com/pod-product-compliance
Lightning Source LLC
Chambersburg PA
CBHW030930180526
45163CB00002B/522